Library of
Davidson College

communicating with a computer

S.M.P. Handbooks
We Built Our Own Computers
Practical Programming by P. N. Corlett and J. D. Tinsley

S.M.P. Handbooks

communicating with a computer

A. B. BOLT
Principal Lecturer in Mathematics
at Saint Luke's College, Exeter

M. E. WARDLE
Senior Lecturer in Mathematics
at Saint Luke's College, Exeter

CAMBRIDGE AT THE UNIVERSITY PRESS 1970

Published by the Syndics of the Cambridge University Press
Bentley House, 200 Euston Road, London N.W.1.
American Branch: 32 East 57th Street, New York, N.Y. 10022
© Cambridge University Press 1970
Library of Congress Catalogue Card Number 73-85713
Standard Book Numbers: 521 07633 1 Clothbound
                             521 09587 5 Paperback

Printed in Great Britain by Jarrold and Sons Ltd, Norwich

contents

acknowledgements	vi
preface	vii
1 the desk calculator	**1**
Addition	3
Subtraction	4
Multiplication	5
Classroom Approach	7
2 programming a desk calculator	**8**
Flow Diagrams	10
Loops	12
Multiplication	14
Division	16
Paper Stores	18
3 the concept of a computer	**20**
Input and Output	22
Arithmetic Unit	27
Store and Control Units	28
4 computer languages	**31**
A 3-address Language	32
Jump Instructions	38
5 the computer and the classroom	**45**
Flow Diagrams	47
Uses for the 3-address Language	49
The Class Computer—a Computer Game	51
6 mathematical applications	**55**
Numerical Processes	55
Square Root	56
Graph Plotting	58
Standard Functions	59
Solution of Equations	60
Evaluating Integrals	62
7 uses of computers	**63**
Payroll	63
Rates and Accounts	64
Electoral Registration	65
Stock Control	66
Management	67
solutions to exercises	**69**
further reading	**77**
index	**79**

acknowledgements

We are grateful to the following firms for permission to reproduce photographs.

International Computers Ltd. (ICL)
 Figures 4, 5(a), 6, 7 and 8 in Chapter 3

The National Cash Register Company Limited (NCR)
 Figures 1 and 5(b) in Chapter 3

British Olivetti Limited
 Figure 1 in Chapter 5

preface

This book has been written from the authors' experience of teaching children from 13 to 18, and lecturing to groups of teachers and student teachers on programming a computer.

It is our belief that the computer is increasingly affecting and influencing the lives of us all. We should therefore make school leavers of all ages aware of the widespread uses of the computer and the problems involved with communicating with such a machine.

The book is written for anyone willing to admit that they know nothing about a computer. It attempts to take the reader in easy stages, by means of many worked examples, diagrams, and exercises, to the point where he can understand what a computer is, what it is capable of doing, and how it can be made to do it. We believe that by starting with a simple desk calculating machine and constructing a symbolic language to describe its use, it is an easy step to come to terms with the principles of a full scale digital computer.

The first chapter has been written for those who have never handled a desk calculating machine before and it explains its use in simple stages. A symbolic language is then developed in the next chapter to describe to an operator how any given arithmetic calculation can be carried out using a desk calculator. At this stage we consider the basic components and the problems of actually communicating with a full scale digital computer.

In Chapter 4 a simple 3-address language, which has much in common with many commercial autocodes, is studied in detail. This is well within the grasp of most 14-year-olds and explains how data is processed within the computer. The logical thought needed here is an excellent mathematical training in its own right.

A chapter has been devoted to the place of computing in the classroom. Many of the existing mathematical topics can be used to impart the knowledge of computing to the pupils, and often these can be enhanced and become more meaningful in this context. Whilst ideally we would like to see a mini-computer in every school, Chapter 5 explains how a 'classroom computer' can be used to simulate the real thing. We have attempted to show how some of the normal mathematical topics are directly linked to this work, but it would take a book in its own right to show, to the full, the possibilities of the computer in school mathematics.

In order to show the value of the computer in today's world, the final two chapters deal with a few of the mathematical, commercial, and everyday applications of the computer.

The main objective of the book is to introduce the concept of a computer and the basic ideas behind programming at a level with which most children can cope. We have deliberately stopped short of the many applications suitable for older pupils, and numerical methods which have been made the subject of several books already.

We hope the readers of this book will treat it as a starting point and increase their knowledge and experience by further reading and, where possible, by using an actual computer.

1 the desk calculator

The average desk calculator, as shown in figure 1 below, is capable of performing to a very good degree of accuracy, quite a number of fairly sophisticated calculations.

We shall, however, only be concerned with the four arithmetic operations, namely addition, subtraction, multiplication, and division. With these we shall see how a sequence of instructions can be built up to describe the various steps in a given calculation.

figure 1   A desk calculator

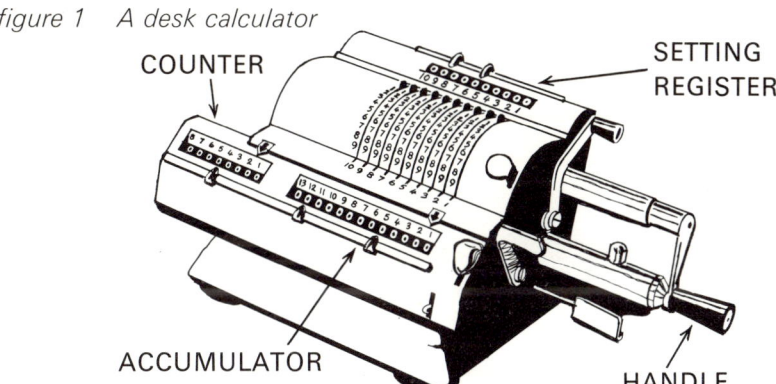

All desk calculating machines of this type will have the same basic properties.

(a) Any number can be entered, or INPUT, into the top right hand window by means of the levers directly below it.
(b) When the handle is turned once in a clockwise direction, a new number will appear in the bottom right hand window.
(c) When the handle is turned once in a clockwise direction, the number in the bottom left hand window will increase by one.
(d) The numbers in each of the three windows may be set independently to zero, by their respective clearance levers.

2 THE DESK CALCULATOR

example Set your machine so that each of the three windows is cleared and move the carriage to its extreme left hand position. The windows should now look like diagram (*a*).

(*a*)

Input a number, say 463, at the right hand end of the top window. See diagram (*b*).

(*b*)

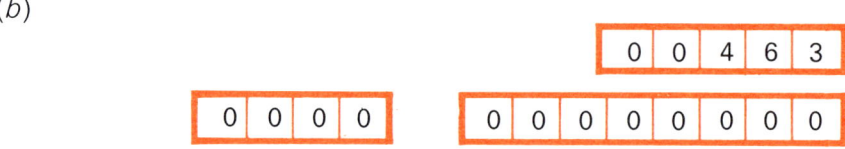

Turn the handle once in a clockwise direction, and the result should be diagram (*c*).

(*c*)

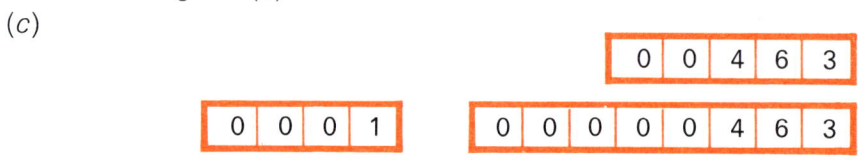

Turn the handle a second time in a clockwise direction, and the result should now be diagram (*d*).

(*d*)

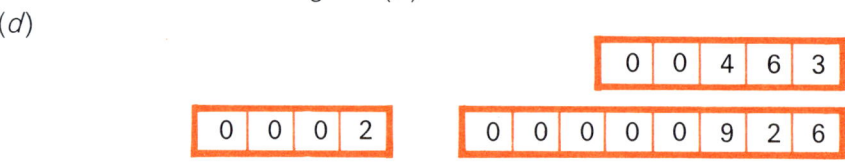

What has been the effect of the above instructions?

The number initially entered has remained unchanged in the top window. After one turn of the handle this number was added into the bottom right hand window. After a second turn of the handle the original number 463 was added to the new contents of the bottom right hand window, giving a result of 926. The bottom left hand window then registered 2, which was the number of times the handle had been turned.

ADDITION 3

At this stage it would be worth denoting each window, or REGISTER, by some appropriate shorthand. The following notation is in fairly common usage.

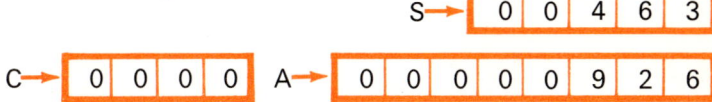

S denotes SETTING REGISTER, A—ACCUMULATOR, and C—COUNTER.

If we wished an operator to do the previous calculation, 463+463, we could summarize the situation with the following sequence of instructions:

> Clear all registers
> Input 463 into S
> Turn handle twice clockwise
> Output result in A

or we could streamline it in this way:

Such a sequence of instructions is called a PROGRAM.

We must realize that an operator will only carry out the actual instructions that he is given. If, for instance, we had omitted the 'clear all registers' instruction, we would be adding the 463 to whatever the previous user of the machine had left in A. Also the 'output A' instruction is necessary in order for the operator to know in which register to find the result of the calculation.

ADDITION

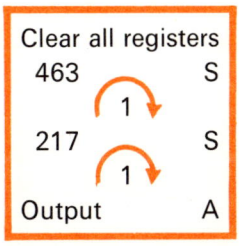

What does this program do?

4   THE DESK CALCULATOR

In the last program, after adding 463 into A we changed S to 217 before turning the handle a second time. This has the effect of adding the 217 now in S to the 463 in A, giving a result of 680 in A.

SUBTRACTION

As ↻ has been taken to mean 'turn the handle clockwise' ↺ could mean 'turn the handle anticlockwise'.

What is the effect of turning the handle anticlockwise?

example

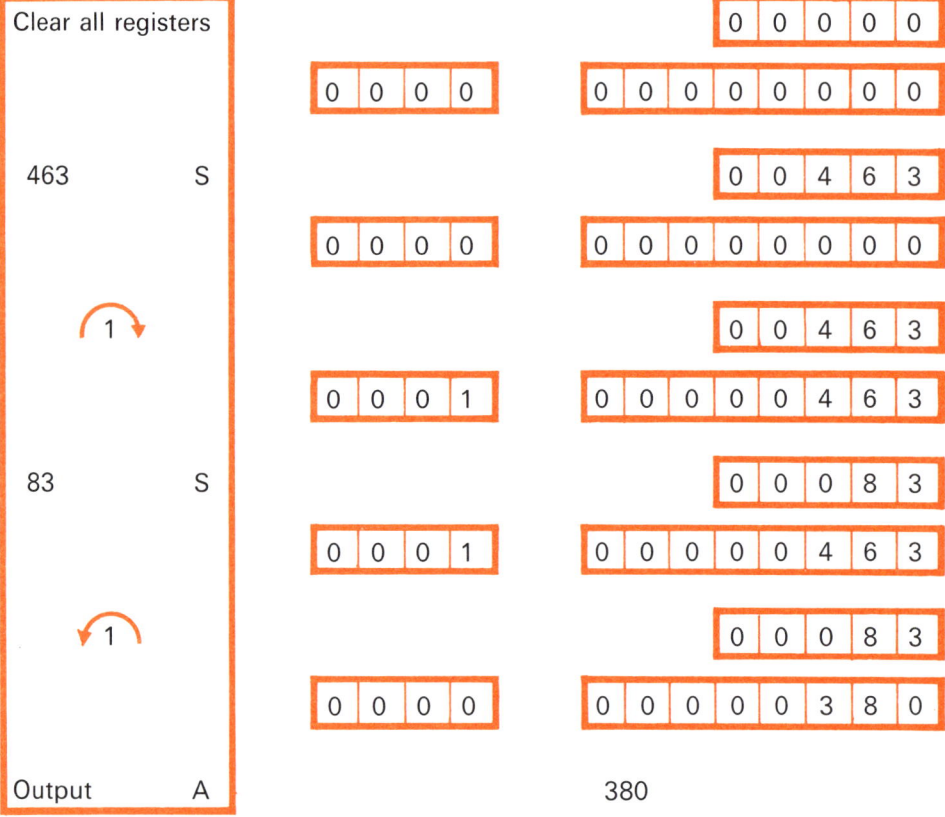

The above sequence of instructions calculates 463−83, and gives a result of 380 in A.

EXERCISE 1

1 What do the following programs do?

(a) 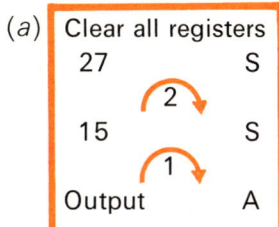 (b) 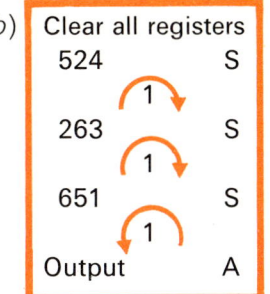 (c)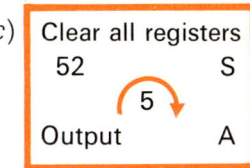

2 Write similar programs for:
(a) 217+519   (b) 413−256
(c) 34+34+34+34   (d) 134+276−192

MULTIPLICATION

3×37

In this program turning the handle three times has the effect of adding 37 into A three times. This is of course the basis of multiplication:

$$3 \text{ times } 37 = 37+37+37$$

Note, the number of times that 37 has been multiplied will be recorded in the COUNTER.

example

(25×7)+(43×4)

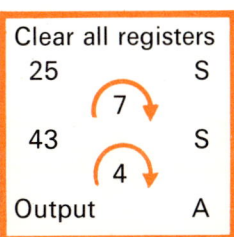

6   THE DESK CALCULATOR

EXERCISE 2

Write programs for:

(a) 261×7   (b) (53×5)+71   (c) (417×23)+479−257

When we wish to multiply by a two-digit number, say 43, it would be extremely tedious to have to turn the handle of the calculating machine 43 times.

We can reduce the number of turns necessary by using the carriage shift facility on the machine.

example   217×43

INPUT 217 into S

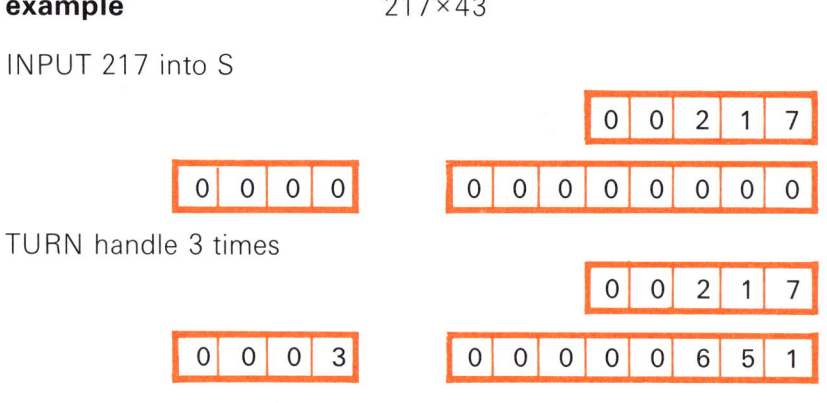

TURN handle 3 times

SHIFT Carriage 1 place RIGHT. (This has the effect of multiplying the number to be added into A by 10)

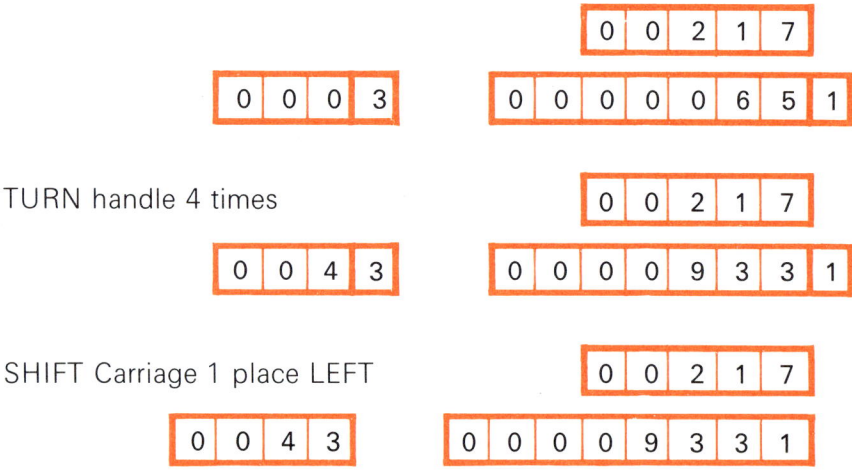

TURN handle 4 times

SHIFT Carriage 1 place LEFT

OUTPUT A: 9331

If we take ⬜→ to mean carriage shift right, the last sequence of instructions could be tabulated as follows:

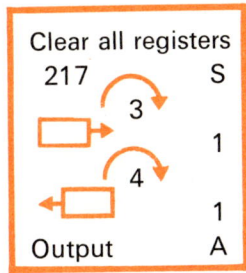

We have now seen several examples of very elementary programs. Note that only those instructions that are given, will be carried out by the operator and one cannot expect him to have read the programmer's mind. He may not insert any extra instructions even though they may seem blatantly obvious.

It is assumed that those readers who wish to develop the use of the calculating machine to its fullest extent, will consult the relevant maker's handbook.

CLASSROOM APPROACH

This work can easily be introduced to children of 11–12, but it is essential that they should have a fairly lengthy session handling a machine, and finding out what they can about it for themselves.

A suitable assignment might be:

Find out all that you can about the machine. Draw a diagram and describe what each handle and lever does. Describe in your own words what you would do to add, subtract, or multiply with the machine.

There is no reason why children should not use their own names for the various registers, and their own symbols for turning the handle and carriage shift. We have used S, A, and C because they have come to be accepted for the more formal programming in the next chapter.

2 programming a desk calculator

In the last chapter we saw how with a few symbolic instructions we could indicate to an operator exactly how to carry out a given calculation. We restricted ourselves to the arithmetic operations, of addition, subtraction, and multiplication.

If we wish to extend our instructions to cope with division and other operations, and also to make full use of the facility of the machine for counting, we need a rather more sophisticated shorthand notation.

In future we shall use the following:

$:=$ to mean 'IS SET EQUAL TO'

therefore INPUT 263 into S becomes $S := 263$
and CLEAR S becomes $S := 0$

similarly, CLEAR A and CLEAR C are $A := 0$, and $C := 0$ respectively.

$S := 16$ would now be read as 'S is set equal to 16'

Instead of ⟲ to represent 'turn the handle' we shall use a pair of instructions stating exactly what takes place in the machine.

$$A := A+S$$
$$C := C+1$$

The effect of the first is to replace A by the sum of the contents of A and the contents of S.

The effect of the second is to replace C by the sum of the contents of C and 1.

In other words the contents of the SETTING REGISTER S are added to the contents of the ACCUMULATOR A, and at the same time the COUNTER C is increased by one.

PROGRAMMING A DESK CALCULATOR

example   A program to add 251 and 473

PROGRAM	NOTES
A := 0	A is set equal to 0 (Clear A)
C := 0	C is set equal to 0
S := 251	S is set equal to 251
A := A+S ⎤	A is set equal to the sum of A and S
C := C+1 ⎦	C is set equal to the sum of C and 1
S := 473	S is now set equal to 473
A := A+S ⎤	A is replaced by 251+473
C := C+1 ⎦	C is again increased by 1
OUTPUT A	724
OUTPUT C	2

There is no need to clear S at the beginning of the program since putting 251 into S erases the previous contents of S.

It may help the construction of a program to make a table showing the contents of each of the three registers after any instruction has been carried out.

example   362+678

PROGRAM		S	A	C
	INITIALLY	?	?	?
A := 0		?	0	?
C := 0		?	0	0
S := 362		362	0	0
A := A+S ⎤				
C := C+1 ⎦		362	362	1
S := 678		678	362	1
A := A+S ⎤				
C := C+1 ⎦		678	362+678	1+1
OUTPUT A			1040	
OUTPUT C				2
OUTPUT S		678		

10 PROGRAMMING A DESK CALCULATOR

In order to subtract one number from another using a machine, it was necessary to turn the handle anticlockwise. This subtracted the contents of S from the contents of A, at the same time decreasing the counter by one.

The pair of instructions for this would be: $\left.\begin{array}{l}A:=A-S\\C:=C-1\end{array}\right]$

example   A program to subtract 371 from 529

PROGRAM	NOTES
A := 0	
C := 0	
S := 529	
A := A+S ⎤	A now holds 0+529
C := C+1 ⎦	C now holds 0+1
S := 371	371 replaces 529 in S
A := A−S ⎤	A now holds 529−371
C := C−1 ⎦	C now holds 1−1
OUTPUT A	158

EXERCISE 3

1 What does each of the following programs do?

(a)	(b)	(c)	(d)
A := 0	A := 0	A := 0	A := 0
C := 0	C := 0	S := 17	C := 0
S := 417	S := 256	A := A+S ⎤	S := 15
A := A+S ⎤	A := A+S ⎤	C := C+1 ⎦	A := A+S ⎤
C := C+1 ⎦	C := C+1 ⎦	S := 19	C := C+1 ⎦
S := 291	S := 147	A := A+S ⎤	A := A+S ⎤
A := A+S ⎤	A := A−S ⎤	C := C+1 ⎦	C := C+1 ⎦
C := C+1 ⎦	C := C−1 ⎦	S := 21	A := A+S ⎤
OUTPUT A	OUTPUT A	A := A−S ⎤	C := C+1 ⎦
		C := C−1 ⎦	OUTPUT A
		OUTPUT A	OUTPUT C

2 Write similar programs for:
(a) 214+376   (b) 199−22   (c) (45×2)−27

FLOW DIAGRAMS

Any sequence of instructions might involve the operator in having to make a decision. If, for instance, he were adding together a number of figures he would be asking the question 'Is there any more data?' If the answer to the question were YES, he would have to input the next bit of data into S. If the answer were NO, he would want to output the result held in A.

Situations of this type can become quite involved, often needing several decisions to be made. It is therefore helpful to organize one's program by using a FLOW DIAGRAM.

In a flow diagram the individual instructions are joined by arrowed lines which indicate the order in which the diagram is to be read.

Because of its possible complexity, it must have a definite START point and also a STOP so that the operator knows when he has finished.

example Calculate the sum of a given list of data and also the total number of items in the list.

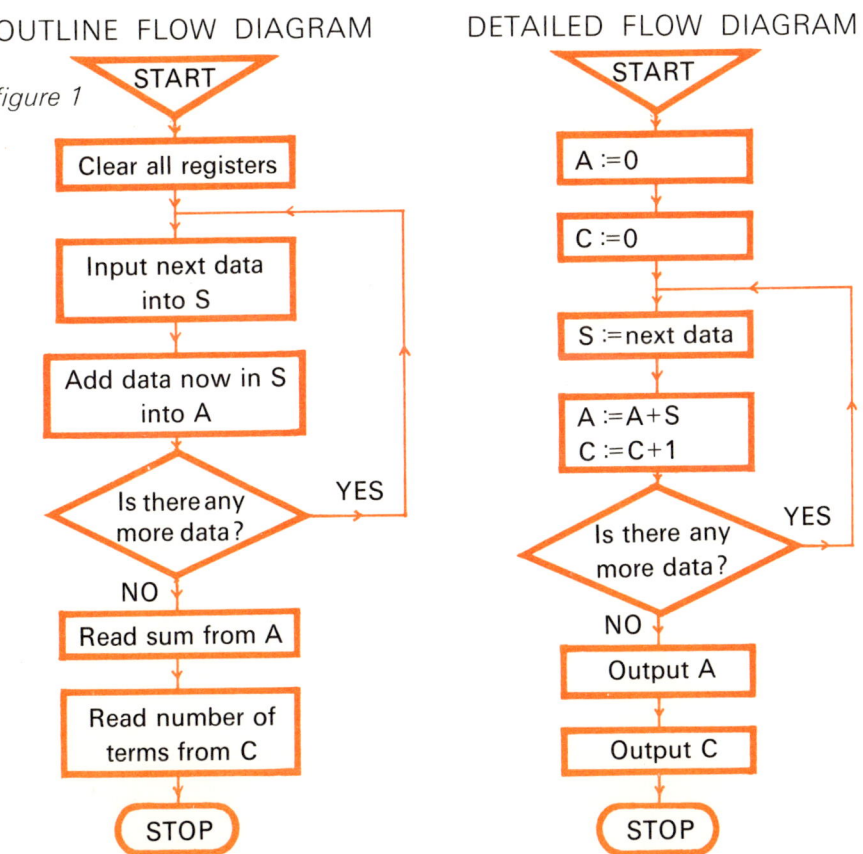

figure 1

12 PROGRAMMING A DESK CALCULATOR

The ▭ boxes are called INSTRUCTION boxes, and the ◇ boxes are called DECISION boxes.

A decision box, for our purposes, may have only two exits. Therefore the questions must be framed to have either the answer YES, or the answer NO.

The exit taken will depend on the answer to the question.

LOOPS

figure 2

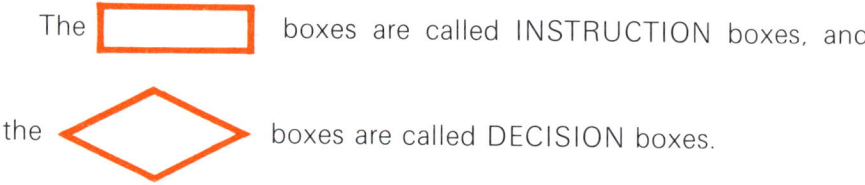

The part of the flow diagram shown in figure 2, where one branch from the decision box rejoins the program at an earlier point, is called a LOOP.

The pair of instructions $\begin{array}{l} A := A+S \\ C := C+1 \end{array}$ is used again and again until the answer to the question is NO.

A loop is a neat way of re-using an instruction or set of instructions within the program.

LOOPS 13

example   A program for 54+54+54+54

We could simplify the flow diagram in figure 3, by using a loop and employing the question 'Is C=4?' The simplified flow diagram is shown in figure 4.

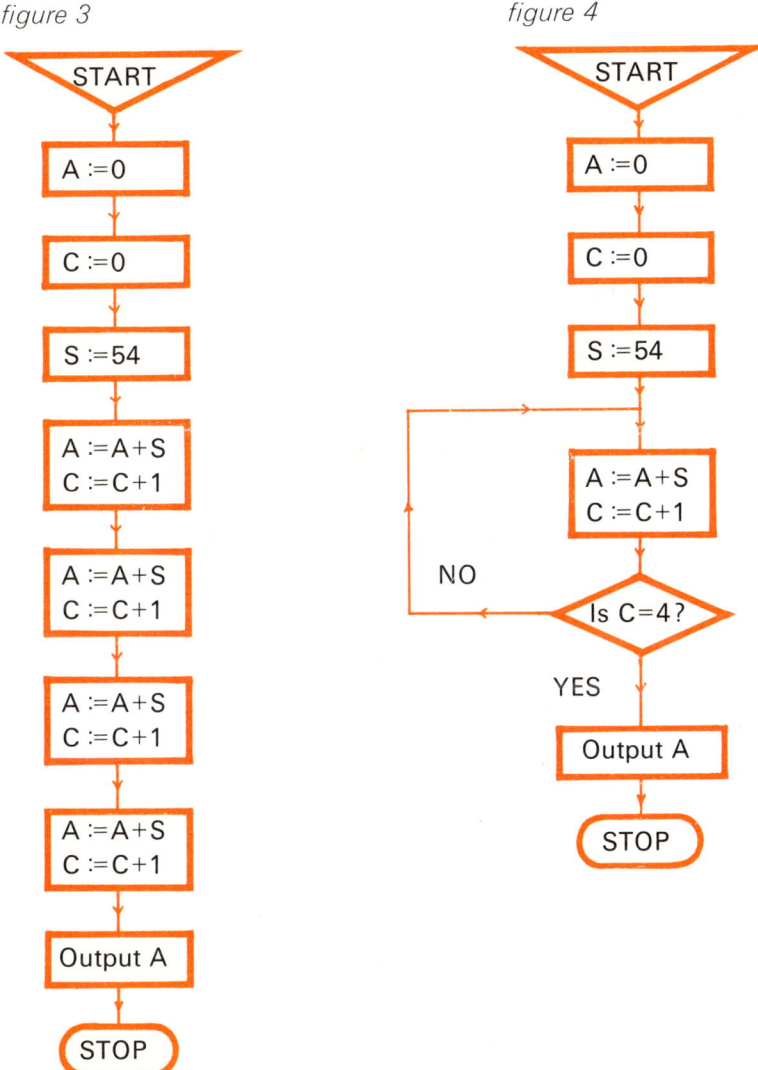

The loop in figure 4 will be cycled until the answer to the question is YES. In this case it will be three times.

MULTIPLICATION

Multiplication is repeated addition. If we wish to multiply 423 by 15, we will add 423 to itself fifteen times.

If S and A are initially set to 423 and 0 respectively, each time we act on the instruction A:=A+S in a loop of our program, 423 is added into A. At the same time, for each cycle of the loop, the instruction C:=C+1 is increasing C by one.

As we wish to add 423 into A fifteen times, we want a test which will tell us when C has increased by 15. If C was initially set to 0, we would ask the question 'Is C=15?' to determine the correct exit to our loop.

example   A program for 423×15

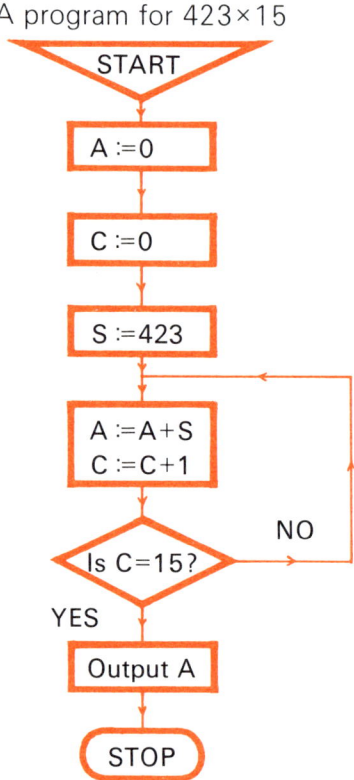

EXERCISE 4

Draw flow diagrams for:
(a) 423+565+217   (b) (725×16)+193   (c) (46×53)+(92×37)

MULTIPLICATION

To ensure that a flow diagram does the required job it is good practice to use a DRY CHECK.

A dry check is a process where a note is made of the result of any given instruction. For each cycle of a loop a different entry will be made and it can then be checked that the exit from the loop is made at the correct time.

example Apply a dry check to the flow diagram for $27^2+(14\times3)$

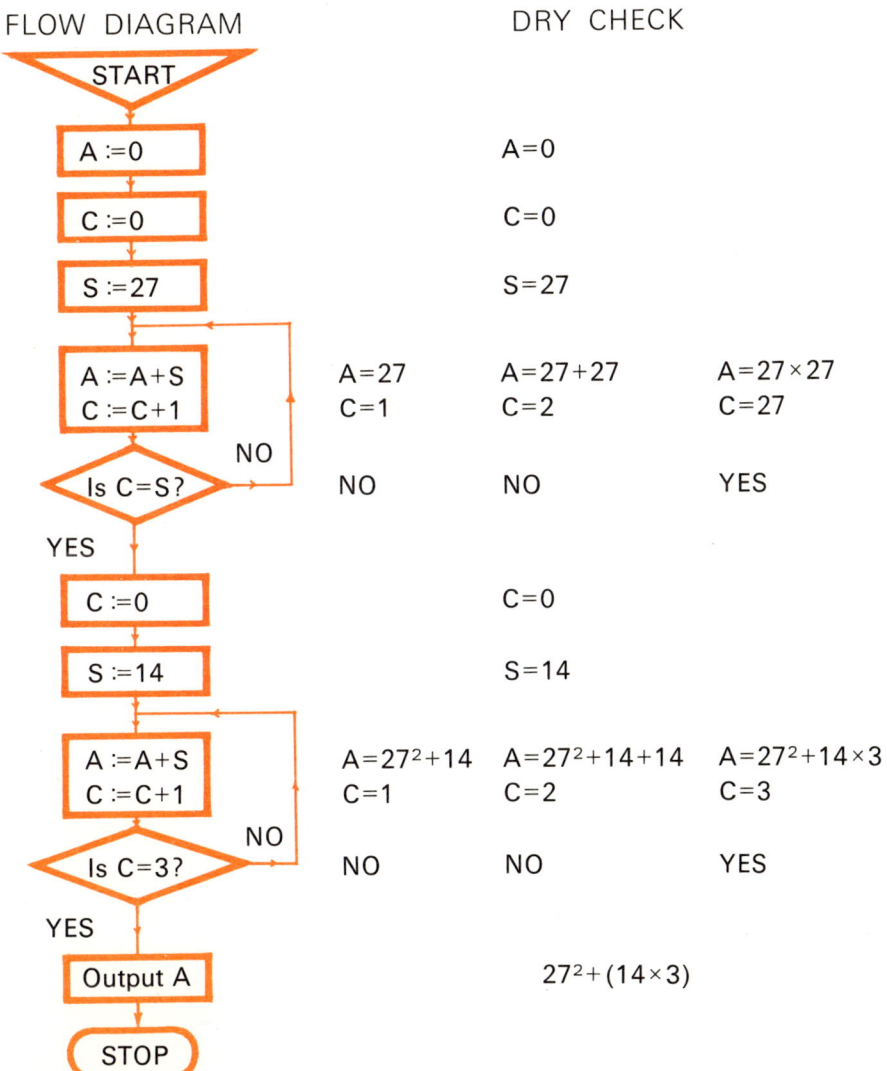

DIVISION

Division can be thought of as repeated subtraction. The divisor is repeatedly subtracted from the dividend until the result is smaller than the divisor. The number of times that the subtraction can be made is counted to give the quotient.

The working for 120÷37 would be:

	Number of subtractions
120	
− 37	
83	1

Is the remainder 83 less than 37? NO.

83	
− 37	
46	2

Is 46 less than 37? NO.

46	
− 37	
9	3

Is 9 less than 37? YES.

This tells us that the remainder is 9, and that the quotient is 3.

The situation is similar to that of the carpenter who wants to know how many 37-inch battens can be made from a piece of wood 10 feet long.

Each time he cuts a piece off, he has to compare the length that is left with that of one of the 37-inch battens. He continues until the length left is less than 37 inches.

In most calculating machines it is possible to arrange for the counter to increase by 1 even when the handle is turned in an anticlockwise direction. The corresponding pair of instructions would be:

$$A := A - S$$
$$C := C + 1$$

DIVISION

example   A program for 120÷37

To divide 120 by 37, we will have to enter 120 into A and 37 into S. We will then subtract S from A until the contents of A are less than the contents of S. The number of times that we have done this will be registered in C.

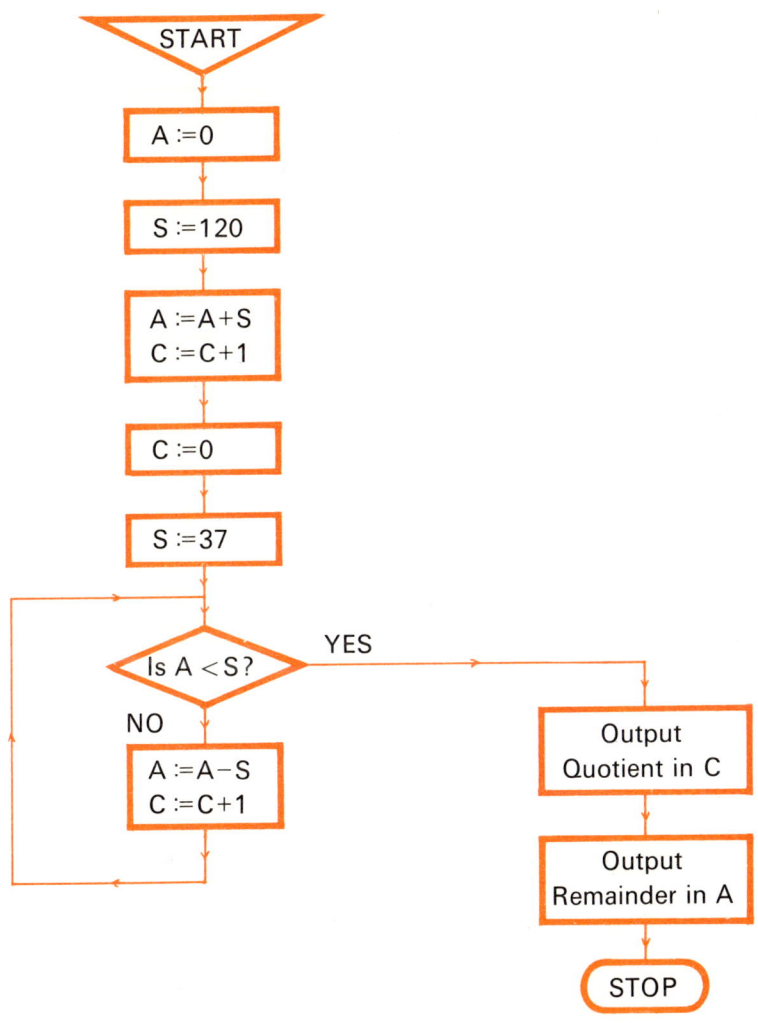

Apply a dry check to this flow diagram to verify that it is in fact correct.

Why is a C:=0 instruction unnecessary at the beginning of this program?

EXERCISE 5

1 Draw flow diagrams for:
(a) $632 \div 43$ (b) $(436+217) \div 19$ (c) $(45 \times 63) \div 13$

2 What calculations are achieved by the flow diagrams in figures 5 and 6?

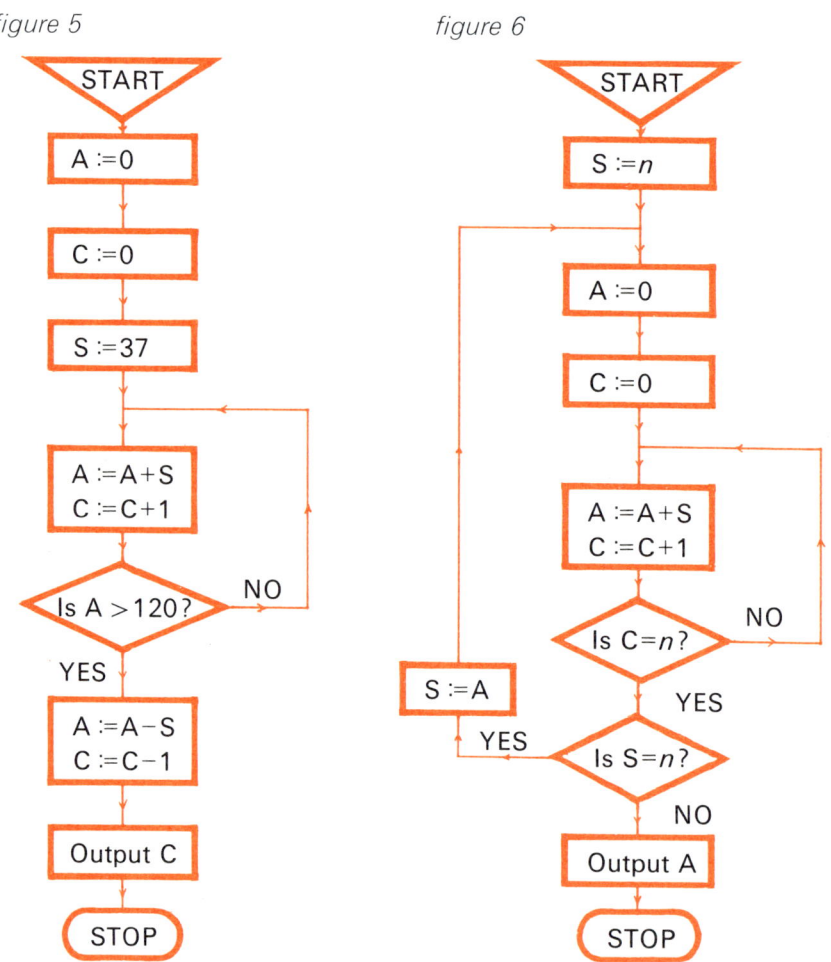

figure 5   figure 6

PAPER STORES

There are many occasions when a calculation can only be carried out if we are allowed to transfer intermediate results from the machine to a piece of paper.

If we need to do this we shall designate certain labelled areas of our paper as PAPER STORES.

When new data is entered in a particular store the previous data held there must be erased. Data may be re-used at a later time by inputting to S from the appropriate store.

example A program to evaluate $\dfrac{143+256}{85-27}$

In this situation before we add 143 and 256, we shall need to transfer, to a paper store P, the result of subtracting 27 from 85.

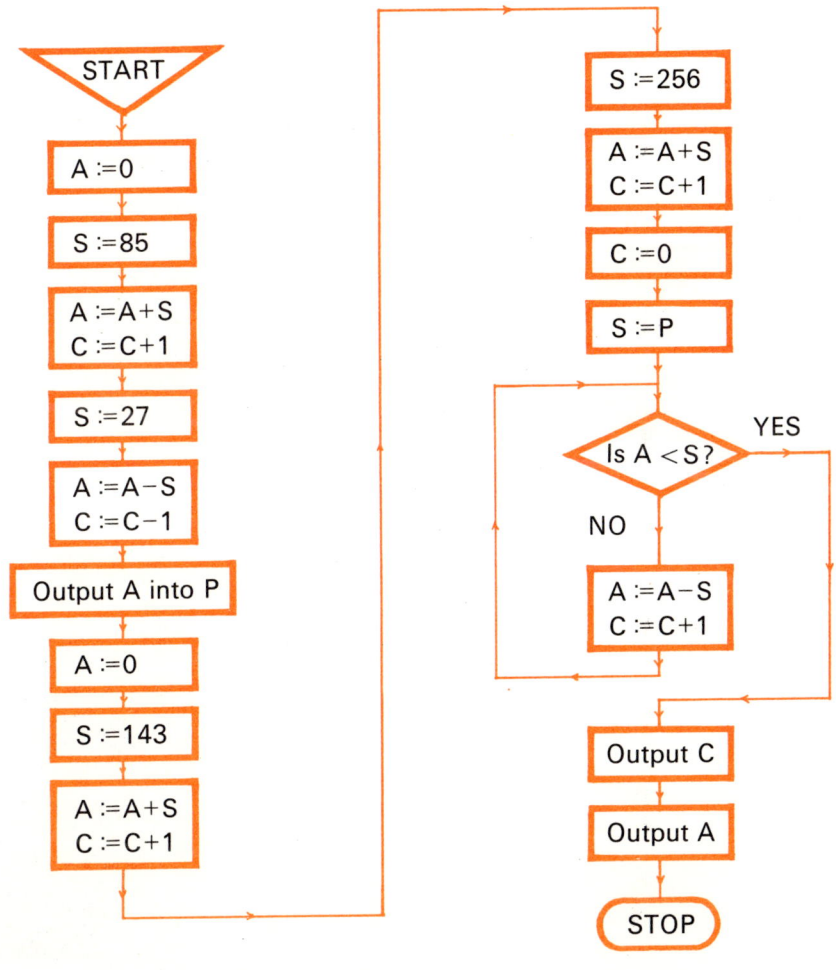

3 the concept of a computer

In the preceding chapters you will have seen how a calculation is carried out using a desk calculator. A modern high speed computer is designed to process numbers in a similar way. There are differences, however, and it is the purpose of this chapter to highlight their similarities and differences.

figure 1 A typical NCR Century System. From left to right—paper tape reader; paper tape punch; integrated printer; printer logic; power supplies; memory; processor console and card input; integrated dual disc unit

[Photograph by NCR]

THE CONCEPT OF A COMPUTER 21

To use either a desk calculator or a computer it is necessary to know:

(a) how to communicate with the calculator or computer;
(b) what calculation is to be performed; and
(c) the data on which it is to be performed.

The way in which a particular calculation is made is much the same in both but the means of communication is very different.

With a desk calculator the operator is in continual contact with the machine and controls every step, using the information he has stored on paper or in his head. At no stage does the calculator work by itself, and the speed with which results are obtained depends to a large extent on the manual dexterity of the operator.

A computer on the other hand does not start to work on the

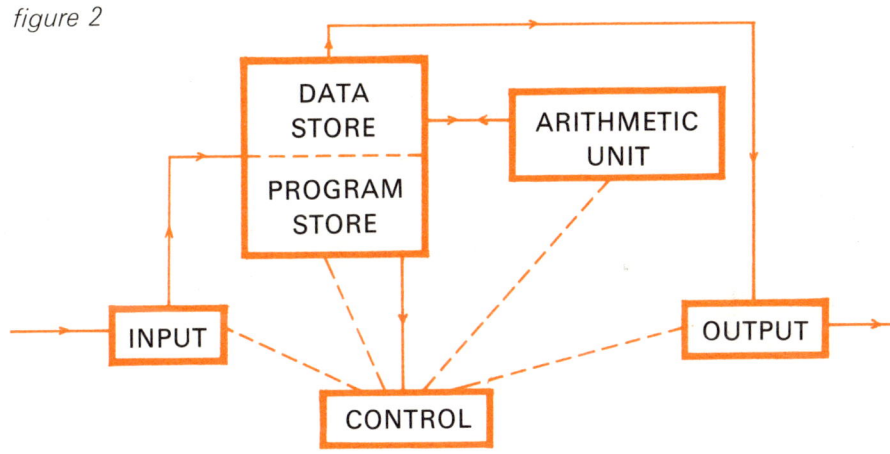

figure 2

calculation until it has stored within itself all the information on how to carry out the calculation. It then 'computes', without human intervention, at very high speed. It is this ability to store the program within itself which distinguishes it from a calculator and has made possible the computer revolution.

Every computer has the same basic design, represented by the block diagram in figure 2. There must be an input unit through which the program and data are fed into the computer, and an output unit where the results of any calculations are made accessible to the operator. In between the input and output units there are, a unit

22 THE CONCEPT OF A COMPUTER

for storing all the available information and the Arithmetic Unit which does any calculations necessary. Coordinating these units is the Control Unit to which the operator has limited access.

INPUT AND OUTPUT

All the information inside a computer is stored magnetically and transferred as electrical pulses. The computer works on the binary principle. It is concerned only with whether a current flows or not,

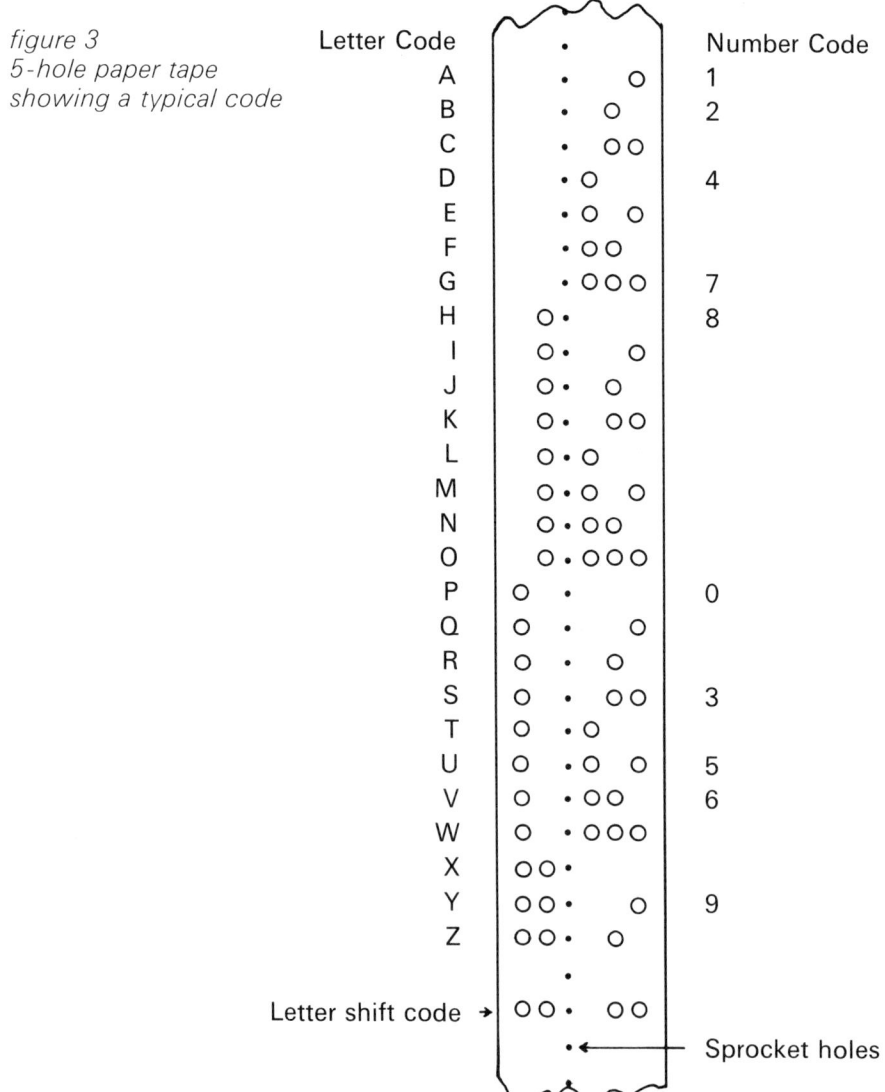

figure 3
5-hole paper tape
showing a typical code

or whether a piece of metal is magnetized or not. Because of this, information has to be supplied to a computer in binary form. No matter what computer language is being used, at some stage in the preparation of the program it has to be converted into a binary form. This is commonly achieved by using punched cards or paper tape, where the presence of a hole in a particular position corresponds to a letter, or a number, or a symbol.

This is not a new idea; punched cards were used in indexing and filing systems long before computers were invented, and cards with

figure 4   Paper tape reader

holes in them are used to control machines in weaving cloth today. Paper tape has been used in teleprinters for some time, while the Morse Code and Braille are common examples of two state or binary systems of relaying information.

The diagram in figure 3 shows how the letters of the alphabet, and each decimal digit, are represented by holes in 5-hole teleprinter tape. The four holes representing 'letter shift' indicate a change from the letter code to the number code or vice versa. This technique enables a pattern of holes to represent more than one symbol—a great advantage.

24 THE CONCEPT OF A COMPUTER

EXERCISE 6

On a piece of tape draw a pattern of holes in teleprinter code corresponding to your car or telephone number. (Assume that the first pattern of holes is in number code unless you precede it with a letter shift pattern.)

The information to be given to a computer may be put onto tape by a tape punch which is not unlike a typewriter to look at. The tape is then fed to a computer through a tape reader. The tape reader illustrated in figure 4 passes the tape across a photo-transistor reading head at 1,000 characters per second. The effect of this is to translate the patterns of holes in the tape into electric pulses inside the computer. (*N.B.* A character is a single symbol such as a letter, or a digit.) Although this is a high input speed it is slow compared to the speed with which information is transferred internally, where it is only limited by the speed at which electricity can travel. If punched cards are used they can be read at speeds of over 1,000 cards a minute and as each card contains 80 characters this compares favourably with the paper tape input.

Because a computer may be unproductive while a program is being fed into it, input speed is important. Therefore a long program is often transferred to a magnetic tape or magnetic disc from which it can be fed in more quickly. The particular type of input used, whether cards, paper tape, or magnetic tape will depend largely on the type of program being handled and the design of the computer system.

The function of the input then is to take the program as written by the programmer and to convert it into electrical pulses inside the computer.

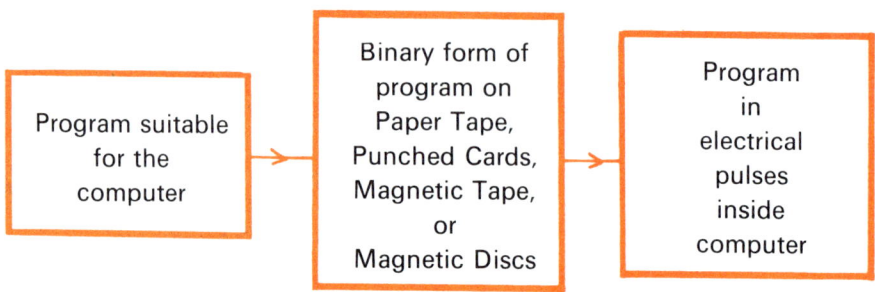

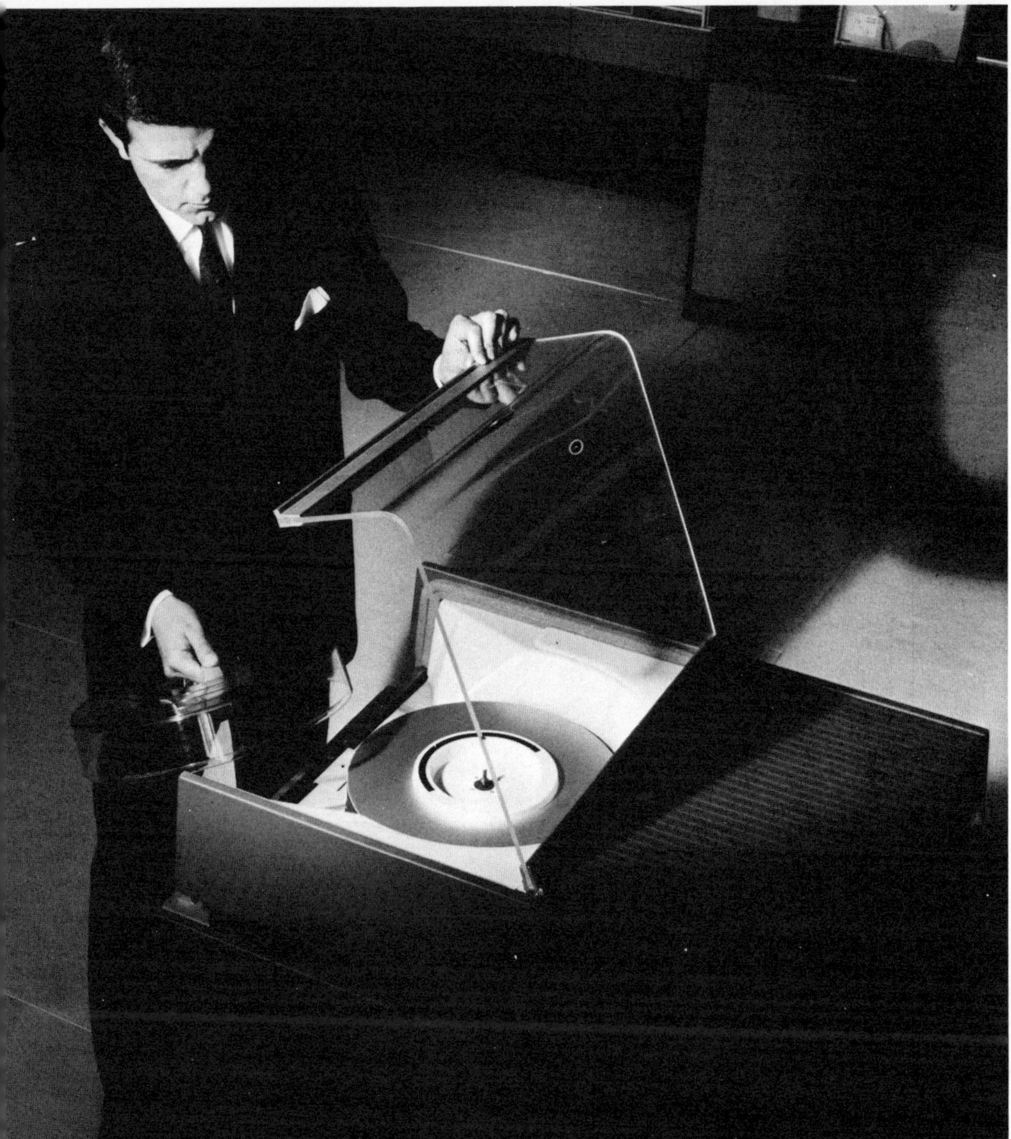

[Photograph by Brindley Muller Associates Ltd]

figure 5(a) Changing a disc-pack

figure 5(b) Magnetic disc read/write heads

[Photograph by NCR]

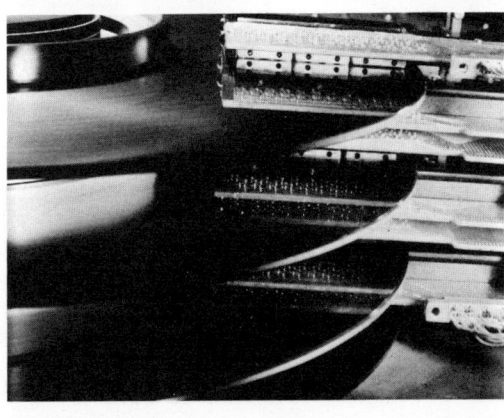

26   THE CONCEPT OF A COMPUTER

The output is essentially the reverse of the input and in its simplest form the electrical pulses inside the computer are translated into holes in cards or tape which are then fed to an electric typewriter which converts them into meaningful symbols on paper.

Input and output devices all come under the general heading of peripheral equipment, for they are not so much the computer itself as the means of access to it. (The sum total of all the units is often called the computer system.) As much time and money has gone into the design of the peripheral equipment as into the computer itself, for the right equipment can greatly enhance the computer's use. Nowadays when you visit a computer system most of the equipment which you see, and certainly the units with most visual impact, are not the computer but the peripheral equipment which makes the computer efficient. The output, for example, may be through a graph plotter which can be watched as it systematically plots points on a

figure 6   Graph plotter

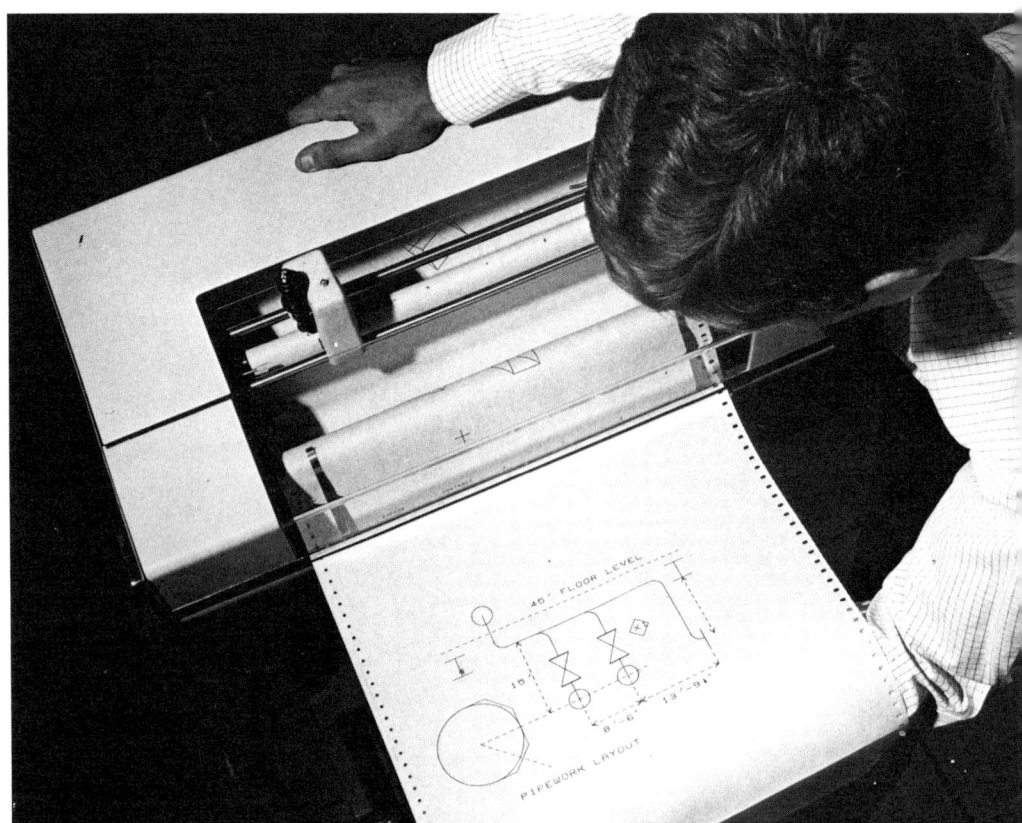

ARITHMETIC UNIT 27

graph to correspond to the solution of an equation. It may be through a line printer which can print, in one minute, over 1,000 lines, each with over 100 characters. Alternatively, a visual display may be achieved on a cathode ray tube.

ARITHMETIC UNIT

This part of a computer corresponds to the desk calculator and is responsible for doing all the arithmetic. (It has been described as the computer's workshop.) Numbers are represented in binary form by patterns of electrical pulses and are operated on by the use of micro integrated circuits at very high speed. One large modern computer, for example, is quoted as capable of adding two numbers together in less than a microsecond or multiplying together two seven-digit numbers in 1·5 microseconds. Putting this another way, the

figure 7 An ICL System. From left to right—*paper tape reader, control desk, magnetic tape units*

[Photograph by Walter Nurnberg]

computer could perform in 1 second more than 1,000,000 additions such as

$$8,627,491 + 9,283,578$$

or perform more than 600,000 multiplications such as

$$2,934,776 \times 5,724,599$$

The mind boggles at such a performance and it becomes clear that the input and output mechanisms must be very efficient in order to satisfy the computer's appetite.

With few exceptions, numbers always enter the arithmetic unit from the store and the result of any calculation is returned to the store.

STORE AND CONTROL UNITS

The store unit is best compared to a vast filing cabinet with thousands of drawers, each of which can hold just one number or one instruction. The drawers are arranged in such a way that each can be easily identified and its contents examined or changed. When a program is fed into the input it is 'loaded' into the store where it will remain until something is done to replace it. Data is stored similarly in the unit and the only distinction between numbers and instructions is in their location.

The control unit takes the program instructions from the store in order, and sets the appropriate parts of the computer to work rather as a conductor of an orchestra following the musical score brings in each instrument at the appropriate time. (In this analogy the composer corresponds to the programmer.) In fact the control unit behaves rather like the operator of a desk calculator following one of the programs in the last chapter. The operator reads an instruction, moves the appropriate parts of the calculator and then looks at the next instruction.

The speed with which an instruction can be located in the store and read determines to a large extent the operational speed of the computer. The design of the store is therefore significant. Most modern computers have a ferrite core matrix store (see figure 8) composed of thousands of circular magnets located at the intersection of a network of wires—each magnet represents a single binary digit.

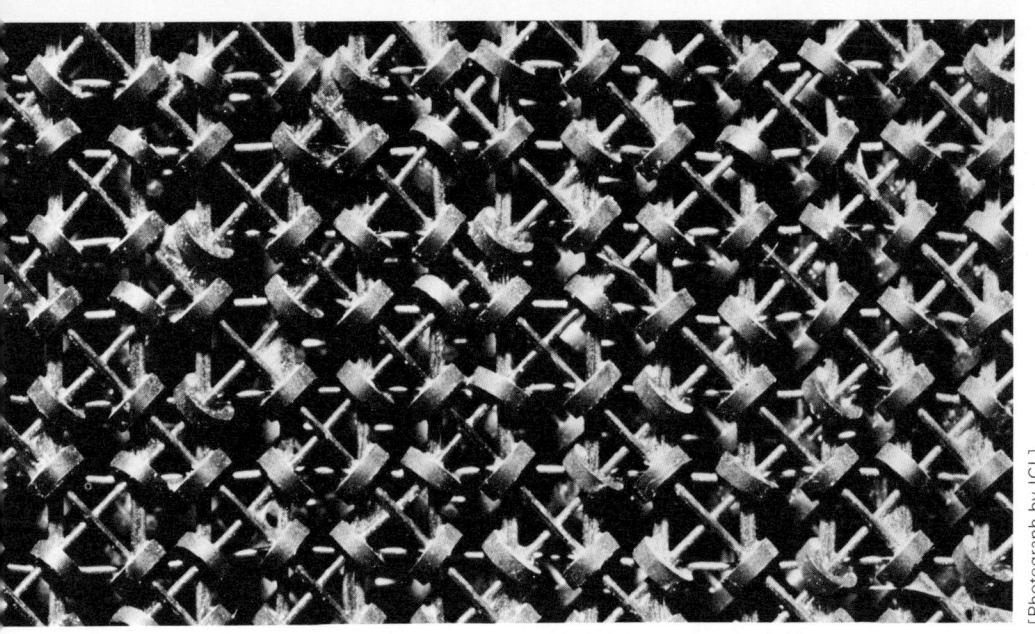

[Photograph by ICL]

figure 8   Close-up of ferrite core matrix store much magnified

Such a store may be described as having a capacity of 32K (one K is a capacity of 1,024 'words' where a word is equivalent to 10 binary digits), and a transfer time measured in microseconds. As we shall see later, the versatility of a computer depends on the capacity of this store.

The way in which a computer system undertakes a task should now be clear and it is summed up in a flow diagram on the next page, in which it is assumed that input is by paper tape.

We hope that the reader now has an overall appreciation of the relation between the different parts of a computer. This understanding can be increased by: further reading (some titles are given at the end of this book); viewing films and television programmes on computers; visiting establishments which have a computer system.

One very good film we would recommend is *Your Obedient Servant* which can be hired from the Central Film Library, Government Building, Bromyard Avenue, London, W.3. This film packs a lot in and needs to be seen several times to be fully appreciated.

When visiting a well organized commercial or scientific establishment to see a computer, the first impression may well be of disappointment, for rows of silent grey boxes belie the fact that any work is being done. The only noise to be heard will be from the air

30 THE CONCEPT OF A COMPUTER

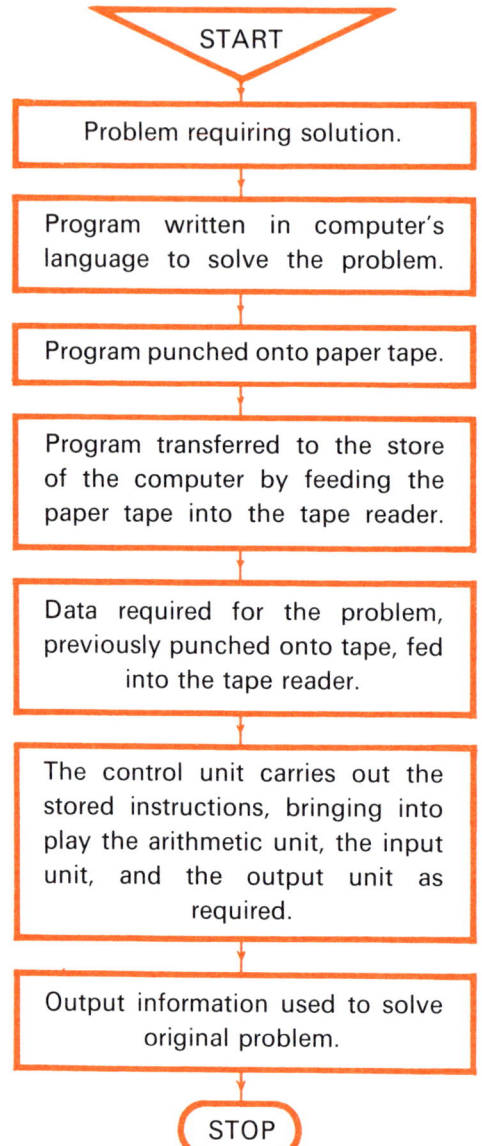

conditioning plant or a tape punch, while the operator may be sitting quietly apparently doing nothing. It is only on looking into adjacent rooms filled with girls preparing tapes or punched cards that one realizes how many people are being served directly or indirectly by the computer and the enormous amount of data processing which has gone on. Disappointment is replaced by awe.

4 computer languages

We discussed in some detail in the previous chapter the way in which the program is fed into or out of a computer, but we have not yet discussed what form the instructions of the program must take.

A computer has a language of its own which depends entirely on the way its designers and engineers made it. This language is of the same kind as the desk calculator language, already discussed, for it must tell the computer in minute detail what to do. Simple additions need several steps while multiplication and division require even more. To write a program for a small calculation in the computer's own language (known as *machine code*) is a very laborious procedure and would soon tax our patience. Fortunately for us, however, the computer designers construct a language (called an *autocode*) in which it is relatively easy for us to write our program, and then arrange for the computer to translate it.

This translation is done by a program called a *compiler* (or interpreter) which is written by the original designers in machine code. The compiler is first fed into the computer and translates any appropriate autocode program which follows into machine code.

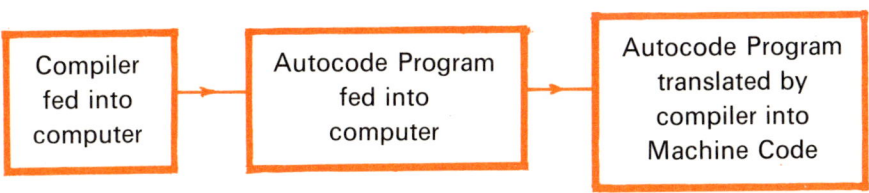

The design of the compiler is very important for the efficient use of the computer with the autocode. It is inevitably a long program, for it must be capable of translating any instruction in the autocode, and because of this it can take up a large proportion of the storage capacity of a small computer. One analogy is that of a language interpreter at the United Nations, while another is that of a foreign language phrase book we might use on a holiday abroad.

By the use of compilers a large computer may be capable of accepting a number of different autocodes. Attempts have been made to have a standard autocode and Algol has been fairly successful although there are probably as many users of Fortran. Any new computer will have compilers designed for both these languages although there is no doubt that before long they will be superseded by better ones. These languages are highly sophisticated, and far removed from the basic machine code of the computer. Hence we have chosen to discuss a simpler language, which has much in common with the earlier autocodes, in the belief that it gives a better understanding of how the computer does its work. (Anyone wanting to learn Algol should consult the book list at the end of this book.)

A 3-ADDRESS LANGUAGE

We saw earlier with a desk calculator how a program could be written by referring to the different registers. Similarly, in this language we want to be able to refer to the different *locations* (the 'drawers') of the computer store. To do this we give each *storage location* an address, one of

$$S1, S2, S3, \ldots, S20$$

This assumes that twenty locations are capable of being addressed and is adequate for our purposes. In practice, however, there would be thousands of addressable locations.

We will now consider the *arithmetic instructions*, for they show clearly why the language is called a 3-address language.

The instruction

$$S2 := S3 + S7$$

tells the computer to look at the numbers stored in S3 and S7, to add them together and then put the result in S2. It has the effect of displacing whatever was in S2, but the contents of S3 and S7 are unchanged as the following example shows.

	S2	S3	S7
Initial content of stores	568·93	91·36	64·01
S2 := S3+S7			
Subsequent content of stores	155·37	91·36	64·01

A 3-ADDRESS LANGUAGE

The next instruction we consider

$$S5 := S3 \times S3$$

has one storage location repeated. It tells the computer to replace the contents of S5 by the square of the number in S3.

The same address can in fact occur in all three places as the next example shows

$$S4 := S4 + S4$$

The instruction tells the computer to add the contents of S4 to itself and put the result back in S4—in other words it doubles the contents of S4.

Any of the arithmetic operations $+$, $-$, $\times$ and $\div$ can be used in these 3-address instructions, and the following example will give you a chance to understand their use.

example At a certain stage when the contents of S1, S2 and S3 are 12, 19 and 31 respectively the computer performed the following sequence of instructions:

$$S1 := S1 \times S1$$
$$S2 := S2 + S3$$
$$S3 := S2 + S2$$
$$S3 := S2 + S3$$
$$S3 := S3 - S1$$
$$S1 := S1 \div S3$$

Find how the contents of these storage locations change.

The best way to ascertain this is to use a table with one column for each store location used and make a 'dry check'.

INSTRUCTIONS	S1	S2	S3
	12	19	31
S1 := S1 × S1	144	19	31
S2 := S2 + S3	144	50	31
S3 := S2 + S2	144	50	100
S3 := S2 + S3	144	50	150
S3 := S3 − S1	144	50	6
S1 := S1 ÷ S3	24	50	6

34 COMPUTER LANGUAGES

EXERCISE 7

Find the contents of S1, S2 and S3, if they initially contained 5, 3 and 21 in that order, after the following sets of instructions:

(a)
S2 := S1 × S2
S3 := S3 − S2

(b)
S3 := S1 − S1
S1 := S2 ÷ S2

(c)
S1 := S2 + S3
S1 := S1 ÷ S2
S3 := S3 ÷ S2
S3 := S3 − S2
S1 := S1 ÷ S3

(d)
S1 := S1 × S1
S1 := S1 − S3
S3 := S3 ÷ S3
S3 := S3 + S3

(e)
S3 := S1 − S2
S3 := S3 × S3
S3 := S3 × S3
S1 := S1 × S1
S2 := S2 × S2

It now remains to consider the *input and output instructions* which are as follows:

$$S5 := \text{Tape}$$
$$\text{and} \quad \text{Print S6}$$

Data to be used in a program is punched on a separate tape and placed in the tape reader. When the computer obeys the first instruction above, it operates the tape reader and whatever number is stored next on the tape is entered into S5. Any storage location can have data entered into it in this way.

The print instruction is self-evident. On obeying this instruction the computer arranges for a teleprinter to type out the contents of S6.

Although numbers are stored inside the computer in binary form this need not concern us here for the computer automatically translates decimal numbers into binary and arranges that its output is also in decimal form. As far as we are concerned the storage locations can be imagined to hold decimal numbers to an accuracy of 8 significant figures and be able to distinguish between positive and negative numbers.

Notice that none of the instructions refer to numbers but only to locations where numbers are held. We are now in a position to write a complete program, and the next example illustrates a program for a straightforward computation.

example Write a program to compute $\dfrac{89 \cdot 46^2 - 23 \cdot 29}{73 \cdot 62}$

The first step is to decide the order in which the numbers in the calculation will appear on the data tape, for this will determine the whole program.

The calculation has then to be broken down into a sequence of binary operations (that is, operations which combine two numbers to give one number), for, like us, a computer cannot handle more than two numbers at a time.

If we let the data be punched onto the tape in the order

1. 89·46   2. 23·29   3. 73·62

a suitable program is as follows:

PROGRAM	NOTES
START	
S1 := Tape	89·46 → S1 ⎫ Where possible the
S2 := Tape	23·29 → S2 ⎬ input instructions come
S3 := Tape	73·62 → S3 ⎭ together at the beginning.
S1 := S1 × S1	89·46² → S1
S1 := S1 − S2	(89·46²) − 23·29 → S1
S1 := S1 ÷ S3	(89·46² − 23·29) ÷ 73·62 → S1
Print S1	Result of calculation printed.
STOP	

The last instruction, STOP, tells the computer that it has come to the end of the program.

Notice that as the program itself does not refer to actual numbers it is really a set of instructions for evaluating the formula

$$\frac{x^2 - y}{z}$$

given the values of x, y, and z.

When writing a program in this language we need to remember that the contents of a storage location will be changed whenever its address appears on the left-hand side of an instruction. Hence if a number stored, say, in S5 is to be used more than once in a calculation, it is necessary to ensure that S5 is only on the right of any instruction in which it appears.

The next example illustrates these points.

example Write a program to evaluate $\dfrac{x^2y+y^2z+z^2x}{x+y+z}$ given x, y, and z.

Punch the data onto the tape in the order:

1. x 2. y 3. z

then the following program will do.

PROGRAM   NOTES
START
S1 := Tape $x \to $ S1
S2 := Tape $y \to $ S2
S3 := Tape $z \to $ S3
S4 := S4−S4   This clears S4 ⎫
S4 := S4+S1 $x \to $ S4   ⎬ S4 used as an
S4 := S4+S2 $x+y \to $ S4   ⎬ accumulator.
S4 := S4+S3 $(x+y)+z \to $ S4 ⎭
S5 := S1×S1 $x^2 \to $ S5
S6 := S2×S2 $y^2 \to $ S6
S7 := S3×S3 $z^2 \to $ S7
S2 := S5×S2 $x^2y \to $ S2 ⎫ x, y, z not needed again
S3 := S6×S3 $y^2z \to $ S3 ⎬ by themselves so stores
S1 := S7×S1 $z^2x \to $ S1 ⎭ re-used.
S2 := S2+S3 $x^2y+y^2z \to $ S2
S2 := S2+S1 $(x^2y+y^2z)+z^2x \to $ S2
S2 := S2÷S4 $(x^2y+y^2z+z^2x)/(x+y+z)$
Print S2
STOP

A 3-ADDRESS LANGUAGE

Why wouldn't it matter in this case if the data were punched on the tape in the wrong order?

The longer a program is, the more room it takes in the program store and the longer it takes to be computed, so one aim in writing a program is to make it as short as possible and to use as few storage locations as possible.

EXERCISE 8

1 Write programs to compute:

(a) $\dfrac{2639 \times 173}{786 - 254}$ (b) $\dfrac{2 \cdot 83^2 - 3 \cdot 96}{2 \cdot 83 + 3 \cdot 96^2}$

(c) What would happen if the data tape was punched in the wrong order?

2 Write a program to compute $1 \cdot 932^5$.

3 Write programs to evaluate the following formulae:

(a) $\dfrac{x+y}{x-y}$ (b) $\dfrac{x^2 y - x + y}{xy}$ (c) $\dfrac{x^2 y^2 + x + y}{x^2 + y^2}$

(d) In one of these the order of the data makes no difference. Which one?

4 Write a program to evaluate the cubic

$$2x^3 - x^2 + x + 2$$

when $x = 2 \cdot 34$.

5 (a) Write a program to find the average of the numbers 8·34, 9·72, 6·41, 7·35.

(b) What is the smallest number of storage locations needed?

6 Write a program to evaluate the determinant

$$\begin{vmatrix} a & b \\ c & d \end{vmatrix}$$

7 Write a program to compute the product of two 2×2 matrices.

JUMP INSTRUCTIONS

In many computing processes a sequence of instructions has to be repeated over and over again. Consider, for example, the following program for adding together three numbers x, y, z.

Data tape 1. x 2. y 3. z

PROGRAM	NOTES
START	
S2 := S2−S2	$0 \to S2$
S1 := Tape	$x \to S1$
S2 := S2+S1	$x \to S2$
S1 := Tape	$y \to S1$
S2 := S2+S1	$x+y \to S2$
S1 := Tape	$z \to S1$
S2 := S2+S1	$(x+y)+z \to S2$
Print S2	
STOP	

After the first instruction the remainder of the program consists of repeating the two instructions

$$S1 := Tape$$
$$S2 := S2+S1$$

The computer is being used as a desk calculator where S1 is used as the setting register and S2 as the accumulator.

Suppose, now, we wanted to use the computer to add together a large amount of data. It would be a very tedious procedure to write out the above two instructions for every number to be added even though this is effectively what has to be performed by the computer. We get around this difficulty by having in our language an instruction such as

If more data jump to (2)

This instructs the computer to go back to the second instruction if there is any more data on the data tape, but to obey the next instruction if there is no more data.

The flow diagram for summing an unlimited number of data and the associated program are shown opposite.

JUMP INSTRUCTIONS

figure 1

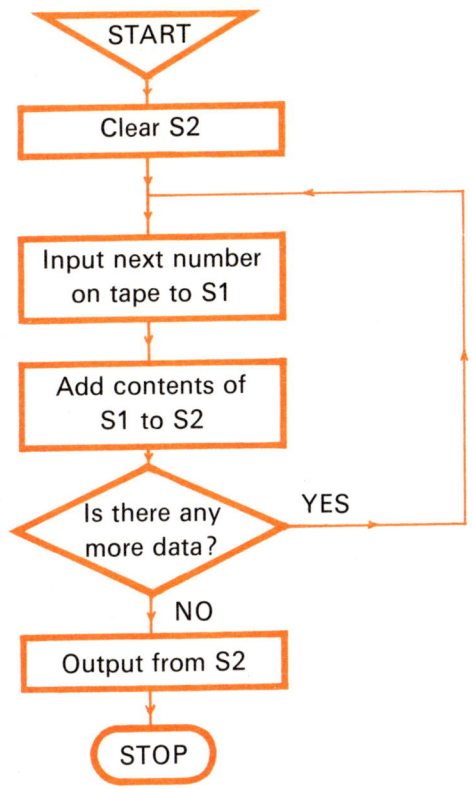

PROGRAM

START
(1) S2 := S2−S2
(2) S1 := Tape
(3) S2 := S2+S1
(4) If more data jump to (2)
(5) Print S2
STOP

loop [brackets instructions (2)–(4)]

NOTES to show similarity to desk calculator

Clear accumulator
Next number input to setting register
Turn handle clockwise

Output number from accumulator

If instructions (4) and (5) are interchanged the program will print out the 'running total' for each new number added.

Do a dry check with some simple data.

If instead of the sum of the numbers we wanted the sum of the squares of the numbers the program could easily be adapted by the insertion of one instruction in the loop as follows:

Loop
- (2) S1 := Tape
- (3) S1 := S1 × S1   Squaring instruction
- (4) S2 := S2 + S1
- (5) If more data jump to (2)

EXERCISE 9

Write a program to find the sum of the cubes of the numbers on the data tape.

Programs for the sums of squares and the sums of products of two sets of numbers are the backbone of many statistical calculations, and once a program has been written, say for a standard deviation, it can be kept and used whenever required as only the data will be different. A library of standard programs is the stock in trade of any computer establishment. The programs are stored on paper tape, magnetic tape or magnetic discs and form what is called the *software* of the computer system.

A desk calculator has an inbuilt mechanism for counting the number of additions or subtractions which have been made to the accumulator and apart from its obvious use in multiplication it has many other roles. Suppose we wish to find the average of a set of numbers, then after adding them together we have to divide by the number of data. This number is clearly given by the counter. With a computer we first have to designate a particular storage location as the counter and then write into our program a set of instructions to make it count. The program which follows is an extension of the summation program to find the average of the data. As each new number is added to the accumulator the contents of S3 is increased by 1 so that it acts as a counter and finally the accumulated total is divided by the number in the counter.

Care has to be taken in clearing the stores to be used as accumulator and counter before the action starts. (To help the writing of programs, the language is so constructed that 0 and 1 can be used in place of a storage location.)

JUMP INSTRUCTIONS

program to compute the sum and the average of a set of numbers

```
         START                NOTES
    (1)  S2 := 0              Clear accumulator
    (2)  S3 := 0              Clear counter
 ┌─▶(3)  S1 := Tape           Number input to setting register
 │  (4)  S2 := S2 + S1        Number added into accumulator
Loop(5)  S3 := S3 + 1         Counter increases by 1
 └──(6)  If more data jump to (3)
    (7)  Print S2             Sum printed out
    (8)  S2 := S2 ÷ S3
    (9)  Print S2             Average printed out
         STOP
```

Another important jump instruction is of the type

(11) If S4 < S1 jump to (7)

This tells the computer to go to the seventh instruction whenever the number in S4 is less than the number in S1. When this is not the case the computer goes to instruction (12).

One use of this instruction, with a counter, is illustrated by the following program which raises a given number to a given power. Notice how care has been taken to ensure that the contents of the counter is equal to the power of the number at each stage.

program to compute a^N given a and N

```
         START                NOTES
    (1)  S1 := Tape           N → S1
    (2)  S2 := Tape           a → S2
    (3)  S3 := S2 × S2        a² → S3
    (4)  S4 := 1 + 1          2 → S4
 ┌─▶(5)  S3 := S3 × S2        Contents of S3 multiplied by a
Loop(6)  S4 := S4 + 1         counter
 └──(7)  If S4 < S1 jump to (5)
    (8)  Print S3
         STOP
```

The following dry check with $N=5$ should make the process clear. Work through it step by step. The contents of a storage location are not repeated if unchanged, but crossed out and the new contents put where appropriate.

Number of instruction	S1	S2	S3	S4	
(1)	5	?	?	?	
(2)		a			
(3)			a^2		
(4)				2	
(5)			a^3		
(6)				$\cancel{3}$	
(7)					$S4 < S1$
(5)			a^4		
(6)				$\cancel{4}$	
(7)					$S4 < S1$
(5)			a^5		
(6)				5	
(7)					$S4 \not< S1$
(8)		Print out a^5			

When the techniques of summation, forming a power and using a counter are mastered they can be combined to write quite complex programs, for they are the building blocks for most mathematical and statistical work.

The use of a loop in a program is very powerful for it is a device whereby the computer can perform many operations after only a small effort by the programmer. Without loops the programmer could never hope to keep pace with a computer's speed.

EXERCISE 10

1 Write programs to compute the following:
  (a) $(3 \cdot 64 + 2 \cdot 98 + 4 \cdot 91 + 3 \cdot 57 + 4 \cdot 35 + 3 \cdot 82)^2$
  (b) $(84^2 + 76^2 + 93^2 + 59^2 + 67^2)(84 + 76 + 93 + 59 + 67)$
  (c) $56 \cdot 4 - 29 \cdot 3 + 45 \cdot 8 - 61 \cdot 2 + 58 \cdot 3 - 52 \cdot 6$
  (d) $1 + \frac{1}{2} + \frac{1}{3} + \frac{1}{4} + \frac{1}{5} + \frac{1}{6} + \ldots + \frac{1}{200}$

JUMP INSTRUCTIONS   43

2 Write a program to determine the least power of 2·6934 to exceed 1,000

3 Work through the following program where the three numbers on the data tape are 100, 3, 3 in that order:

```
      START
(1)   S1 := Tape
(2)   S2 := Tape
(3)   S3 := Tape
(4)   S4 := 1
(5)   S2 := S2 × S3
(6)   S4 := S4 + 1
(7)   If S2 < S1 jump to (5)
(8)   Print S4
      STOP
```

Lines (5)–(7) form a loop (indicated by the bracket from (5) to (7)).

What meaning can you attach to the number computed?

4 An approximation to π can be found from the fact that

$$\frac{\pi}{4} = 1 - \frac{1}{3} + \frac{1}{5} - \frac{1}{7} + \frac{1}{9} - \frac{1}{11} \ldots$$

Write a program to compute an approximation to π using the first 2,000 terms of the series. (*Hint:* Use a counter which increases in steps of 2 and deal with two terms at a time.)

5 A data tape is punched with the two sets of numbers

$$x_1, x_2, \ldots, x_{100} \text{ and } y_1, y_2, \ldots, y_{100}$$

alternately in the order

$$x_1, y_1, x_2, y_2, x_3, y_3, \ldots, x_{100}, y_{100}.$$

Write a program to compute

$$(x_1^2 + x_2^2 + \ldots x_{100}^2)(y_1^2 + y_2^2 + \ldots y_{100}^2)$$

and

$$x_1 y_1 + x_2 y_2 + \ldots x_{100} y_{100}$$

6 A civil engineering contractor estimates that the total cost, £T, of repairs for a machine in n years is given by

$$T = \frac{C(R^n - 1)}{R - 1}$$

where £C is the cost of repairs in the first year, and $R = (1 + \frac{r}{100})$ where $r\%$ is the increase in repair costs per annum.
Write a program to compute T.

5 the computer and the classroom

There are many ways in which a knowledge of computing can be imparted to our pupils and it is the express purpose of this chapter to relate the discussion so far to the classroom.

At the sixth-form level this book could be assimilated as it stands with ease and there are plenty of books and opportunities for sixth formers to pursue their particular interest. It is the years before this

figure 1 Pupils at Sir George Monoux Grammar School, Chingford, using the Olivetti Programma 101 for initial training in computer programming

and those who will never enter a sixth form that we are chiefly concerned with. One important problem though, at all levels, is how to give our pupils time on a computer to try out their own programs. It is only by doing this that they will appreciate the disciplines as well as the art of programming.

Many solutions to the problem have been tried. A small number of schools have been given second-hand commercial computers. Some schools have a data link with a university or education authority computer while others have arrangements to take their programs to a local establishment, or send them by post. On the whole we consider all these solutions unsatisfactory, for: the autocode used is usually far removed from the machine code; most pupils are incapable of writing programs which justify time on a large computer; the time lag between writing a program and testing it is often long; too much time is spent in punching and editing cards and tapes.

We see the best solution for the future to be a small portable computer which can be taken into a classroom and used by the pupils, there and then, by themselves. The Olivetti Programma 101 with its magnetic card program input and printed output, although designed for commercial use, goes a long way towards fulfilling this. It has been used by secondary children of all ages with great success and has even been tried in a junior school (see figure 1). IBM have taken the problem seriously and produced a small number of experimental computers especially designed for the classroom with visual output on a standard television screen which promises to be excellent. Within ten years we could see mini-computers as common in schools as the film projector is now.

At the present, however, most schools do not have ready access to a computer. What can be done? A start can be made very early by using desk calculators as elaborated in the early chapters of the book or even before that with children in the way in which they learn their tables.

The diagram shows a 'times' machine and another machine capable of performing the four binary arithmetic operations. Imaginary machines like this can raise all sorts of questions but at the same time they encourage a dynamic way of thinking about mathematical processes which helps in an appreciation of computers.

figure 2

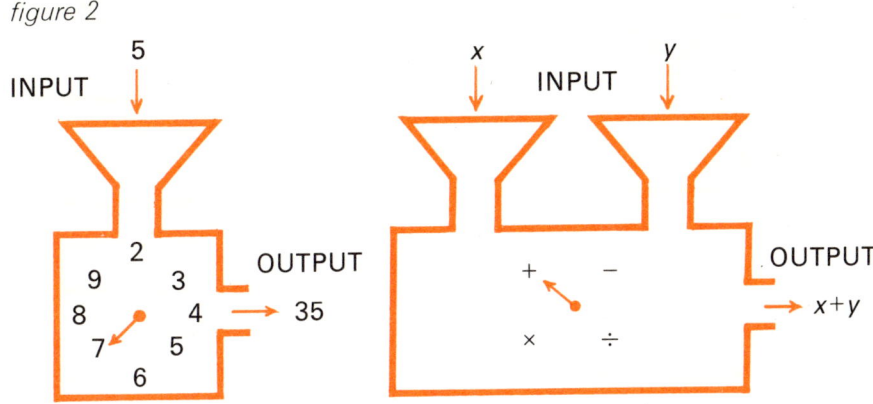

Binary arithmetic (as distinct from binary operations) has perhaps been overstated or wrongly stated. Too many people think that to use a computer you must be able to do binary arithmetic. The computer works in binary but to program it we need know nothing of this. There is little point in becoming highly proficient at doing binary arithmetic. What is more important is to see the way in which information can be represented in binary form by comparing the uses of punched cards, punched tape, morse, traffic lights, and so on. It is possible to show how simple electrical switching circuits can be used to represent binary arithmetic and this can lead on to a discussion of two-state logic and Boolean algebra at a later stage. Two books which give some ideas on these topics at the right level are: *We Built our own Computers* and *Some Lessons in Mathematics*.

FLOW DIAGRAMS

An essential background to all computing is the ability to handle a flow diagram. Experience of following given flow diagrams or constructing their own can be given in non-mathematical situations at an early stage. The knowledge gained of decision boxes, branching, and loops is invaluable to the organization of a program. Flow diagrams can be drawn for such things as: crossing the road, using the telephone, starting a car, laying a table for lunch . . . the possibilities are endless. In figure 3(a) one way is shown of preparing for a bath while figure 3(b) shows how to knit the welt for a sleeve of a child's jumper.

48 THE COMPUTER AND THE CLASSROOM

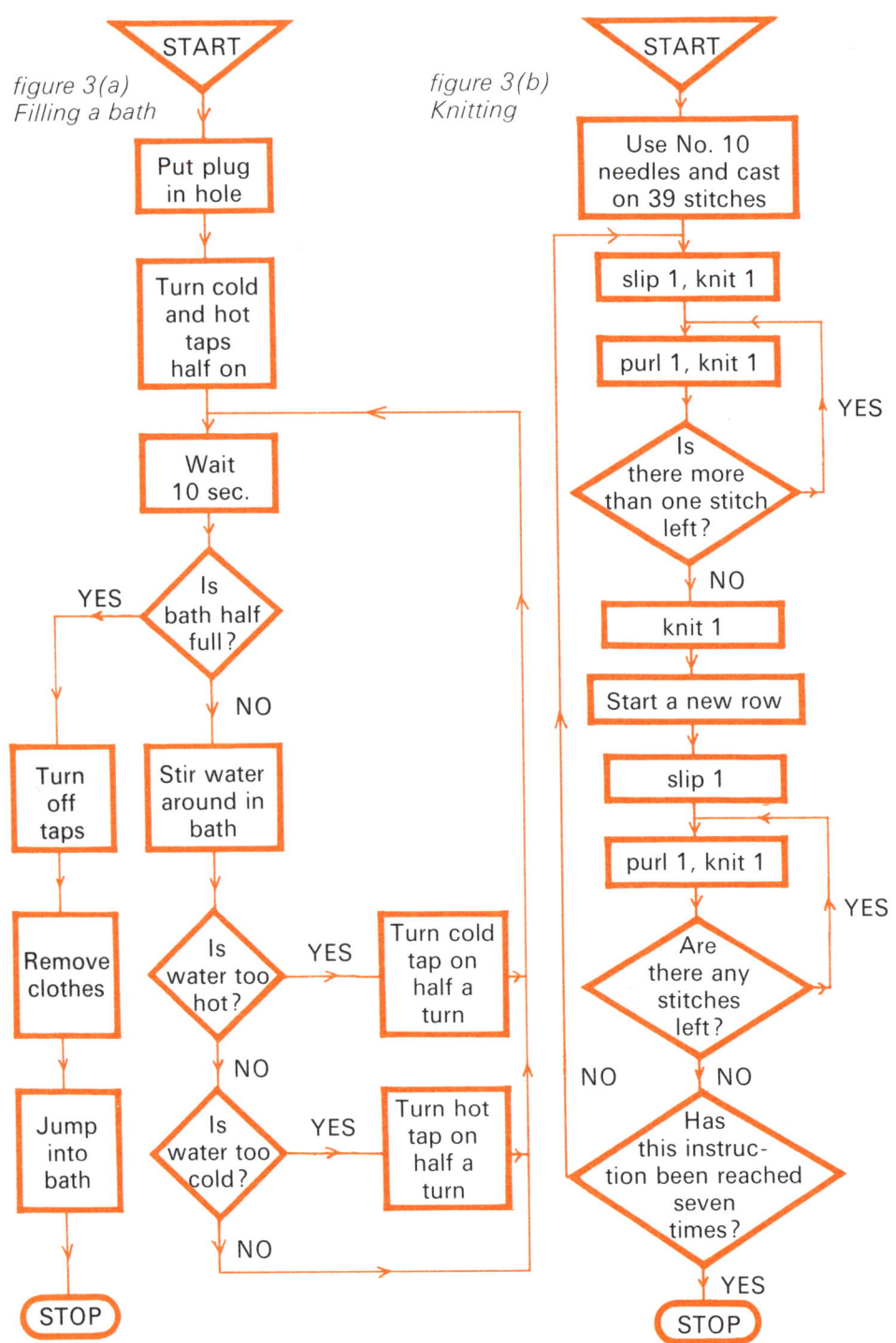

figure 3(a) Filling a bath

figure 3(b) Knitting

The pattern from which the flow diagram was drawn read as follows:

'Using No. 10 needles, cast on 39 sts.
1st row Sl.1, K1, * P1, K1, rep. from * to last st., K1.
2nd row Sl.1, * P1, K1, rep. from * to end.
Rep. 1st and 2nd rows 7 times.'

Most women and girls seem to be able to read such patterns with ease and yet it represents a symbolic language for giving precise instructions to the knitter of a kind similar to the language for a computer program. It is no wonder that girls often make good programmers.

USES FOR THE 3-ADDRESS LANGUAGE

By the third year in a secondary school, most children are capable of simple programming and the 3-address language described earlier has been used by the authors in various forms over several years with success. Two useful school references here are: *The School Mathematics Project, Books 3, 4,* and *Mathematics—A New Approach, Book 4.* By Mansfield & Bruckheimer.

There is no need to bring in jump instructions initially and the input instruction can be simplified by putting, for example,

$S1 := 2 \cdot 34$ instead of $S1 :=$ Tape where $2 \cdot 34$ is on tape.

This enables a quicker start to be made and the use of a separate data tape can be discussed later.

Often children who can adequately use the four rules of arithmetic will be 'stumped' when faced with a calculation such as

$$(36 \cdot 5 + 28 \cdot 4)^2 - 396 \cdot 9$$

or the evaluation of a formula such as

$$\frac{4}{3} \pi r^3$$

The reason is that they are not capable of breaking down the calculation into a sequence of binary operations. This may be because they do not understand the symbolism or just take fright at the sight of all the numbers. Writing a program to evaluate a calculation or formula like the above lays the emphasis on the sequence of simple operations which are needed, and helps the understanding of the process. If a pupil can write a program for evaluating a formula then, subject to his ability to perform the four rules, he should have no difficulty in evaluating the formula given suitable data—it will just be a case of working through his own program.

Writing programs to find the power of a number, when no jump instructions are used, leads to all kinds of ingenious programs based on the pupils' mastery of the index laws. Asked to write a program for computing a^{29}, for example, some pupils will want to write a long program which amounts to them seeing a^{29} as 29 alphas multiplied together. Other pupils will realize that, having achieved a^2, they can produce a^4, a^8, a^{16} by repeated squaring and can then achieve a^{29} as $a \times a^4 \times a^8 \times a^{16}$. A better method still would be to see a^{29} as $a^{32} \div a^3$ and this program is given below with yet another method. A question like this set to a class would lead to an interesting discussion of the different methods which will further their appreciation of indices and number patterns.

	START	NOTES		START	NOTES
(1)	S1 := a	$a \to$ S1	(1)	S1 := a	$a \to$ S1
(2)	S2 := S1 × S1	$a^2 \to$ S2	(2)	S2 := S1 × S1	$a^2 \to$ S2
(3)	S1 := S2 × S1	$a^3 \to$ S1	(3)	S1 := S1 × S2	$a^3 \to$ S1
(4)	S2 := S2 × S2	$a^4 \to$ S2	(4)	S3 := S1 × S1	$a^6 \to$ S3
(5)	S2 := S2 × S2	$a^8 \to$ S2	(5)	S3 := S3 × S1	$a^9 \to$ S3
(6)	S2 := S2 × S2	$a^{16} \to$ S2	(6)	S1 := S3 × S3	$a^{18} \to$ S1
(7)	S2 := S2 × S2	$a^{32} \to$ S2	(7)	S1 := S1 × S3	$a^{27} \to$ S1
(8)	S2 := S2 ÷ S1	$a^{29} \to$ S2	(8)	S1 := S1 × S2	$a^{29} \to$ S1
(9)	Print S2		(9)	Print S1	
	STOP			STOP	

Programs written by the teacher can be worked through by the pupils using a slide rule, desk calculator or any other aid to calculation and have proved a useful motivation for what might otherwise be dreary revision. This can be made really alive and teach a lot about how a computer works if the pupils in the class take on roles as different parts of a computer.

THE CLASS COMPUTER—
A COMPUTER GAME

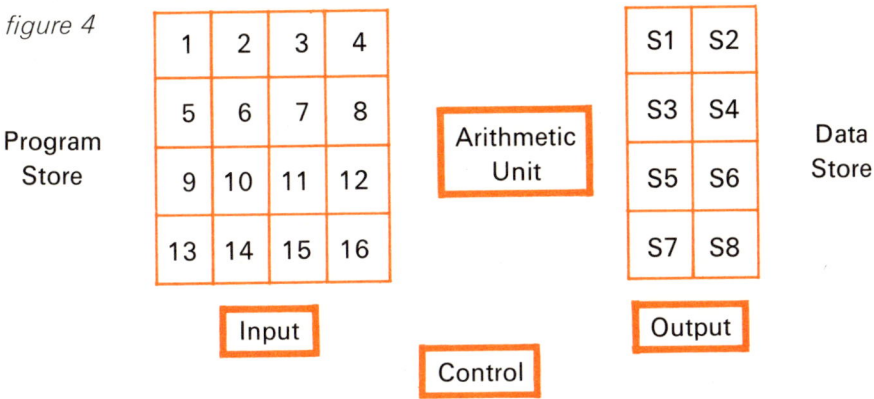

figure 4

A class computer can be designed to suit one's circumstances but the one to be described here has been found a good starting point. The main parts of the computer are shown in figure 4. The program is written in a 3-address language with each instruction on a separate card to compare with a punched card input.

input One pupil is designated as the input and his function is to accept the cards which are given to him, one at a time, and pass them on to the relevant storage location.

program store This has to hold all the instructions of any program used. Either one pupil, or one for each storage location, is designated the program store. He or they will have a set of numbered postcards on which the incoming instructions will be written in order. Any previous instruction existing on the cards will be crossed out when a new instruction is entered.

data store One pupil is needed for each addressable storage location of S1, S2, S3, ... which is likely to be used. Each pupil will have a card clearly labelled with his address, and on the reverse side will be written the number stored by that location. When a new number is entered he will cross out the old number.

Both for the program and data stores a set of 'magic slates' would be ideal, for any previous information stored would be genuinely replaced.

arithmetic unit This will consist of one or two pupils armed with some computational aid such as a desk calculator or a slide rule. They will also need pencil and paper.

output One pupil with a batch of cards on which to write any output data, one number per card.

control One person, almost certainly the teacher initially, to co-ordinate the separate parts of the 'computer'.

Information inside the computer will travel as sound waves! In other words, by word of mouth. Alternatively a 'silent' computer can be achieved by using runners to take written messages between the different parts. The former is more interesting because it helps the participants to understand what is going on.

To use the computer a suitable program followed by the relevant data is written onto a set of cards, one instruction per card. The computer operator then gives these, in order, to the *input* who dictates them one at a time to the *program store* until he has read the instruction, STOP. Nothing further happens until the operator tells the *control* to GO. The *control* then takes the instructions from the *program store* in turn and reads them aloud, leaving time for each to be carried out before continuing. If it is an input instruction, *input* reads aloud the number on the next data card before him and this will be copied by the *storage location* which will have been alerted by *control*. If it is an output instruction *output* will copy the number to be output from the relevant *storage location* and give it to the computer operator. If it is an arithmetic instruction such as

$$S2 := S3 \times S4,$$

the *arithmetic unit* first copies down the instruction, then calls for the numbers from S3 and S4 before doing the necessary calculation and sending the result to S2.

A jump instruction will be carried out by *control*, for the next instruction he obeys will depend on it.

We can hardly describe this as a *high speed* digital computer but it will certainly help to teach a basic understanding of how a computer operates. The first programs tried should be interesting without overtaxing the arithmetic unit, and the one below for generating cubes from a difference technique is suitable.

THE CLASS COMPUTER — A COMPUTER GAME

program to generate a sequence of cubes

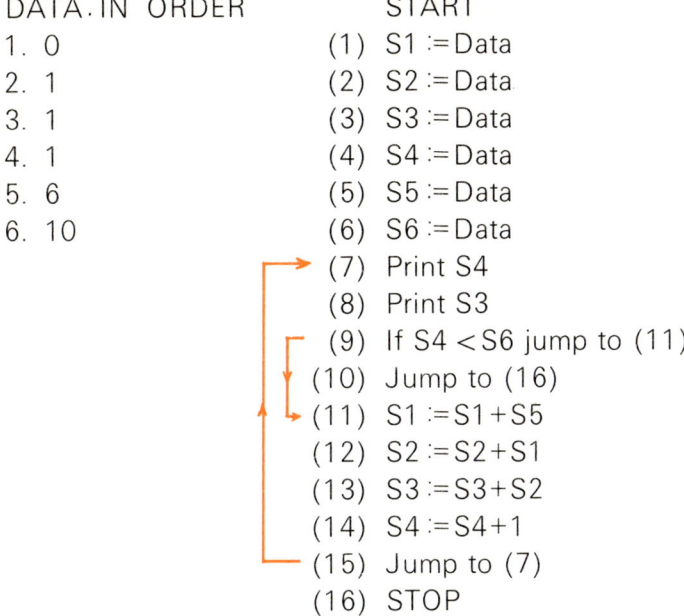

DATA. IN ORDER
1. 0
2. 1
3. 1
4. 1
5. 6
6. 10

START
(1) S1 := Data
(2) S2 := Data
(3) S3 := Data
(4) S4 := Data
(5) S5 := Data
(6) S6 := Data
(7) Print S4
(8) Print S3
(9) If S4 < S6 jump to (11)
(10) Jump to (16)
(11) S1 := S1 + S5
(12) S2 := S2 + S1
(13) S3 := S3 + S2
(14) S4 := S4 + 1
(15) Jump to (7)
(16) STOP

Notice that the input instruction uses the word 'Data' instead of 'Tape'. This is done as the input is with cards.

A new jump instruction also occurs twice. It does not depend on a condition, and whenever the computer reaches it, it automatically jumps to the instruction indicated.

For example, after
                    (15) Jump to (7)
the computer obeys instruction (7).

How does the computer get out of this loop?

Run through a dry check of this program to see how it works before attempting it with a class.

An output instruction occurs inside the main loop so there will be sufficient numbers coming out to keep the 'computer' interested.

Another interesting program is one for Hero's iterative square root process (see page 56) where it can be arranged to output the successive approximations to the square root of any number fed in.

There is a lot to be said for getting a class computer to work through a program without telling them beforehand what it is doing so that they are obliged to 'work in the dark'.

The main difficulty found with a class computer has been to stop its individual parts thinking. It is not on for a humble storage location to spot a mistake by the arithmetic unit! A computer must only do what it is told, no more and no less.

6 mathematical applications

In the previous chapters we have seen how we can communicate with a computer.

We shall now look at some of the mathematical applications and see how the computer has made them possible.

NUMERICAL PROCESSES

One of the greatest facilities of a computer is to produce the results of any given problem to whatever degree of accuracy is required.

example By using the fact that the ratio of successive terms in a Fibonacci Sequence tends to the Golden Section, write a program to calculate its value correct to 6 decimal places.

As we require the ratio to an accuracy of 6 decimal places, we want to compare each new ratio with the previous one and continue until the difference between them is less than say 0·0000001.

In other words we want to incorporate a test into our program which asks the question:

Is | New ratio − Old ratio | < 0·0000001 ?

We need the modulus sign | |, since at any given moment we have no idea which of the two ratios is the larger.

We must therefore allow an instruction in our program, of the type

S1 := |S1|

This is in fact possible since the modulus merely removes the negative sign if there is one.

In the program that follows we have taken a and b as the first two terms of a Fibonacci Sequence. They are punched on the data tape in that order.

MATHEMATICAL APPLICATIONS

PROGRAM   NOTES

     START
(1) S1 := Tape $a \to S1$
(2) S2 := Tape $b \to S2$
(3) S3 := S1 ÷ S2 $a \div b \to S3$
(4) S4 := S1 + S2   New term $a+b \to S4$
(5) S5 := S2 ÷ S4   New ratio $\to S5$
(6) S6 := S5 − S3   New ratio − Old ratio $\to S6$
(7) S6 := |S6| Positive value of S6 $\to S6$
(8) If S6 < 0·0000001 jump to (13)
(9) S1 := S2 $b \to S1$
(10) S2 := S4 $a+b \to S2$
(11) S3 := S5   New ratio replaces Old ratio
(12) Jump to (4)
(13) Print S5   Result
     STOP

Apply a dry check to this program taking $a=1$ and $b=2$.

SQUARE ROOT

One facility which every computer allows is that of taking the square root of a number. Before we utilize the instruction S1 := $\sqrt{S1}$ we ought to realize precisely what is involved.

example Find the square root of 12 correct to 3 decimal places.

The method used by the computer is based on the one discovered by Hero. Since the computer has no idea beforehand what number it will be asked to find the square root of, it is programmed to take as its first approximation, half of the number given.

The working would be as follows:

1st approximation x_1 $12 \div 2 = 6$ $12 \div x_1 = 2$
2nd approximation x_2 $\tfrac{1}{2}(6+2) = 4$ $12 \div x_2 = 3$
3rd approximation x_3 $\tfrac{1}{2}(4+3) = 3·5$ $12 \div x_3 = 3·428$
4th approximation x_4 $\tfrac{1}{2}(3·5+3·428) = 3·464$ etc.

In general

$$x_{r+1} = \tfrac{1}{2}\left(x_r + \frac{12}{x_r}\right)$$

SQUARE ROOT

Hero's method converges very rapidly, and because of its repetitive nature it can be programmed quite simply. The following flow diagram summarizes the situation.

OUTLINE FLOW DIAGRAM

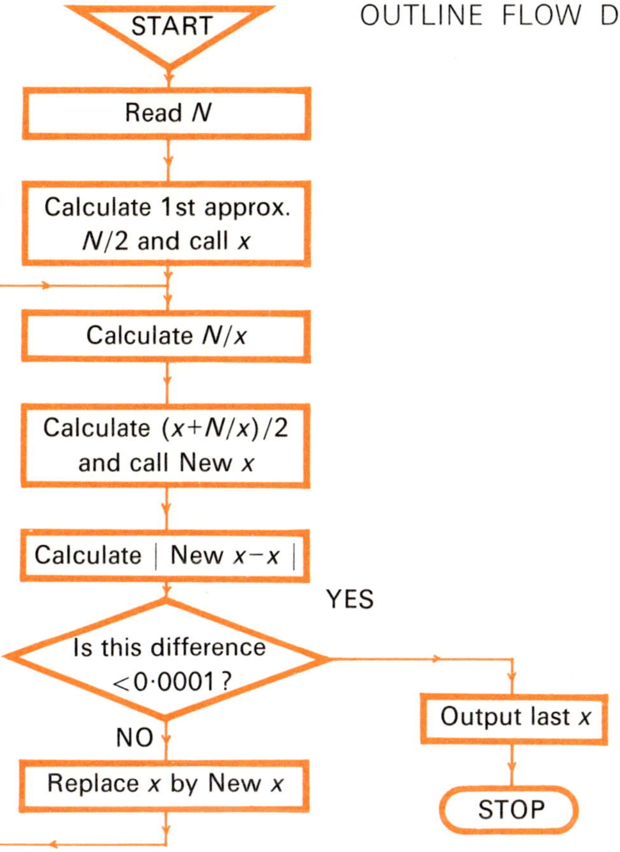

```
START
  ↓
Read N
  ↓
Calculate 1st approx.
N/2 and call x
  ↓
Calculate N/x
  ↓
Calculate (x+N/x)/2
and call New x
  ↓
Calculate | New x−x |
  ↓
Is this difference <0·0001?
  YES → Output last x → STOP
  NO ↓
Replace x by New x
(loop back)
```

The following program would be written into the compiler and would be carried out when an instruction of the type S1 := $\sqrt{S1}$ is met.

PROGRAM

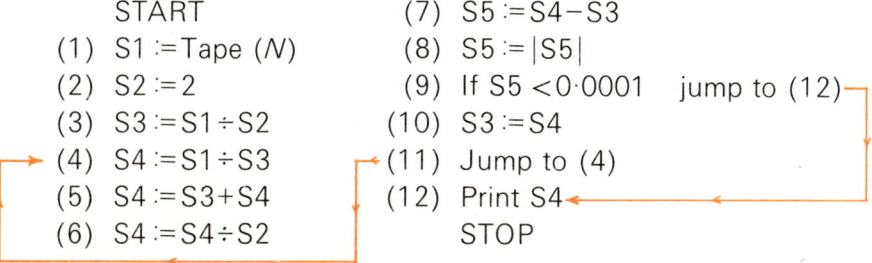

```
        START                (7)  S5 := S4−S3
   (1)  S1 := Tape (N)       (8)  S5 := |S5|
   (2)  S2 := 2              (9)  If S5 < 0·0001  jump to (12)
   (3)  S3 := S1÷S2          (10) S3 := S4
→  (4)  S4 := S1÷S3          (11) Jump to (4)
   (5)  S4 := S3+S4          (12) Print S4
   (6)  S4 := S4÷S2               STOP
```

GRAPH PLOTTING

When we are asked to plot the graph of a mathematical expression we are really being asked to calculate the values of the dependent variable y for a given set of values of x.

We therefore need a program to evaluate y for any given x.

example A program to evaluate $y=ax^2+bx+c$ for integral values of x between 0 and 10.

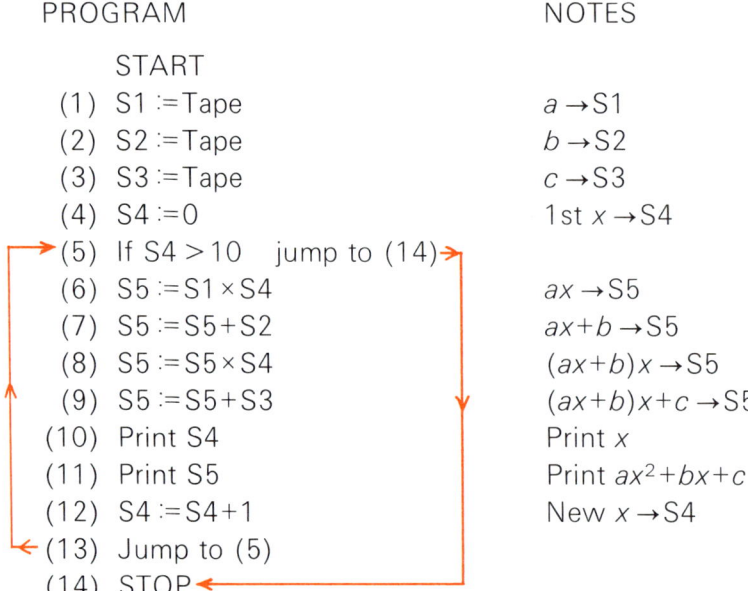

PROGRAM	NOTES
START	
(1) S1 := Tape	$a \to$ S1
(2) S2 := Tape	$b \to$ S2
(3) S3 := Tape	$c \to$ S3
(4) S4 := 0	1st $x \to$ S4
(5) If S4 > 10 jump to (14)	
(6) S5 := S1 × S4	$ax \to$ S5
(7) S5 := S5 + S2	$ax+b \to$ S5
(8) S5 := S5 × S4	$(ax+b)x \to$ S5
(9) S5 := S5 + S3	$(ax+b)x+c \to$ S5
(10) Print S4	Print x
(11) Print S5	Print ax^2+bx+c
(12) S4 := S4 + 1	New $x \to$ S4
(13) Jump to (5)	
(14) STOP	

We can extend this program to evaluate a polynomial of any degree, merely by inputting the relevant number of coefficients and extending the nested multiplication. For example in a cubic,
$$ax^3+bx^2+cx+d \equiv [(ax+b)x+c]x+d.$$

If we wished to consider a varied set of x values listed on the data tape, we would amend instruction (4) to read 'S4 := Tape', instruction (5) to read 'If no more data jump to (14)', and delete instruction (12).

With a modern computer it is possible to plot the x and y values directly onto a graph. The output in this case would be a Graph Plotter, as mentioned in Chapter 3, rather than a Line Printer.

STANDARD FUNCTIONS

Most common mathematical functions such as sin x, log x, and e^x can be expressed as power series in x.

In theory we could store a complete set of tables, but even to 4-figure accuracy these would take up far too much of the available data store.

In practice we evaluate the required function by taking enough terms of the appropriate power series to cover the accuracy needed.

example A program to obtain successive terms and an approximate value for e^x by using the first 100 terms of the series,

$$1+x+\frac{x^2}{2!}+\frac{x^3}{3!}+\frac{x^4}{4!}\ldots$$

PROGRAM

```
        START
  (1)   S1 := Tape    (x)
  (2)   S2 := 1
  (3)   S3 := 1
  (4)   S4 := 1
  (5)   S4 := S4 × S1
  (6)   S4 := S4 ÷ S2
  (7)   Print S4
  (8)   S3 := S3 + S4
  (9)   S2 := S2 + 1
 (10)   If S2 < 100   jump to (5)
 (11)   Print S3
        STOP
```

Programs for common functions such as these, are part of the standard library of programs as issued by the manufacturer of each computer.

They are known as SUBROUTINES and may be called on directly in most languages by an instruction such as S2 := sin (S1). This will automatically replace the contents of store S2 by the sine of the number held in store S1.

We have seen in the last three examples that it is possible to program a computer to evaluate almost any mathematical expression.

SOLUTION OF EQUATIONS

Let us now consider the problem of solving equations. Not only can we program a computer to do this far more quickly than a mathematician with pen and paper, but often we can solve, to a remarkable degree of accuracy, equations which hitherto have been impracticable to solve by traditional methods.

example Find an approximation to the value of the real root of the equation $x^3+x-1=0$

This equation may be rewritten as:

$$x(x^2+1)-1=0 \quad \text{or} \quad x=\frac{1}{1+x^2}$$

The root may be considered as the point of intersection of,

$$y=x \quad \text{and} \quad y=\frac{1}{1+x^2}$$

A process to find this root is suggested by the diagram in figure 1.

figure 1

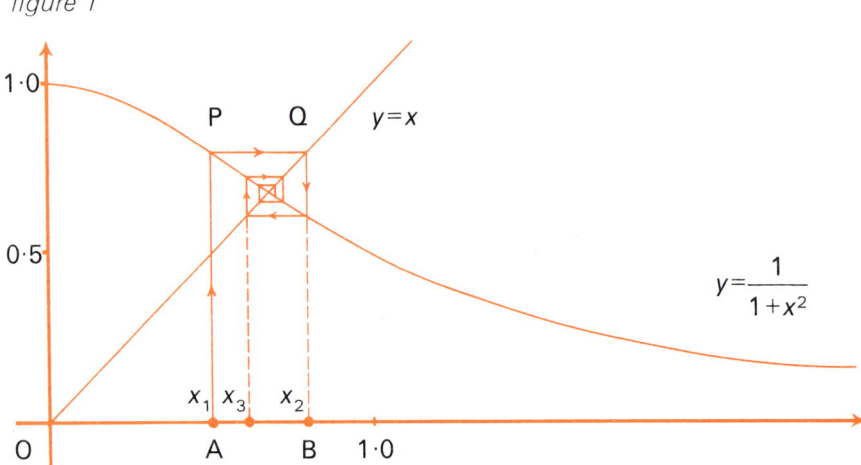

Since $AP=BQ=OB$, each value of $\frac{1}{1+x^2}$ gives us the next approximation for x.

We know that the root lies between 0 and 1 since the values of the original expression at these points are −1 and +1 respectively. If we take our first approximation x_1 to be 0·5, the working would be as follows:

When $x_1 = 0·5$ $\quad \dfrac{1}{1+x^2} = \dfrac{1}{1·25} = 0·8$

when $x_2 = 0·8$ $\quad \dfrac{1}{1+x^2} = \dfrac{1}{1·64} = 0·61$

when $x_3 = 0·61$ $\quad \dfrac{1}{1+x^2} = 0·728$ and so on.

It must be pointed out that before this method can be used, it has to be checked that the way in which the equation has been rewritten does in fact give a convergent process.*

Any process like this, or the method we used for square roots, in which the first approximation is manipulated to give a better approximation is known as an ITERATIVE PROCEDURE.

These together with others, such as Newton's method and the method of False Position,* are typical of a large number of iterative procedures, and could be summarized with the following flow diagram.

AN ITERATIVE PROCEDURE

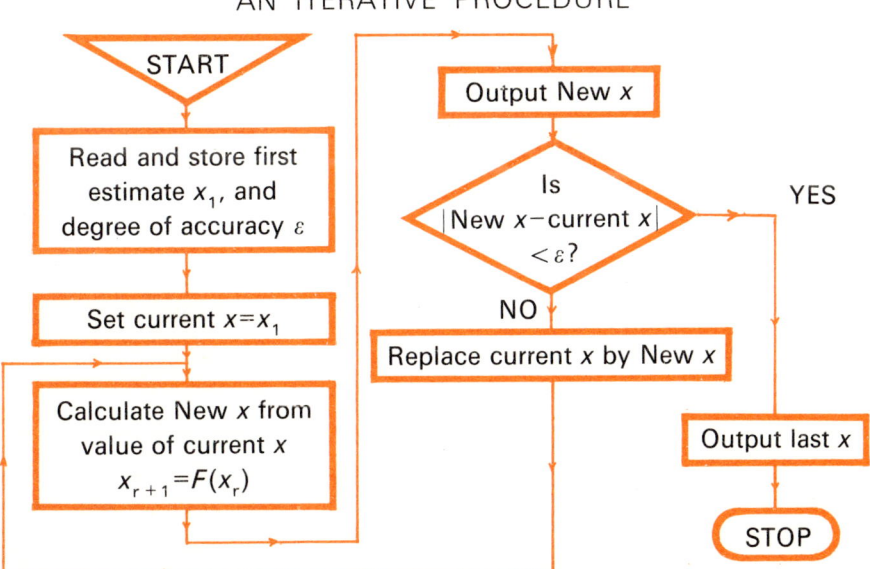

* Ref: *An introduction to Computational Methods* by K. A. Redish.

EVALUATING INTEGRALS

Because of the ability of the computer to do a large number of calculations in a very short time, any convergent integral can be evaluated by one of the many numerical methods such as the Trapezium rule, or Simpson's rule. Providing we take a sufficiently small interval between successive ordinates, the accuracy can be made as great as we like.

This has meant that we can now evaluate those integrals which in the past we have been unable to do analytically.

One simple method, the Mid-Ordinate rule, is shown in figure 2.

figure 2

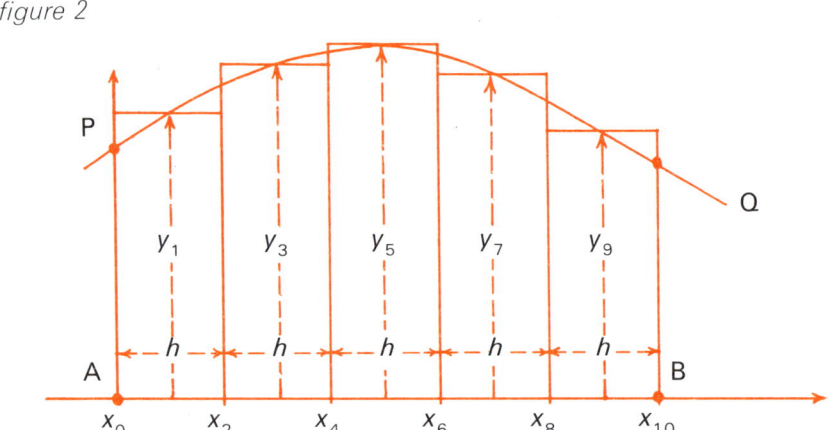

The area APQB is approximately $h(y_1+y_3+y_5+y_7+y_9)$.

Perhaps the two most important applications of mathematics that have been made possible by the modern digital computer, are those concerning the solution of differential equations, and the solution of a system of linear equations. (For the latter, see Chapter 7 under Management.)

A large number of the problems met in scientific and industrial work can be expressed in terms of differential equations. In the past we have been unable to solve a large number of these, but now by using iterative procedures,* and the computer to do the vast amount of calculation necessary, it has been possible to obtain results to a very high degree of accuracy.

* Ref: *An introduction to Computational Methods* by K. A. Redish.

7 uses of computers

The variety of uses to which computers are now put is staggering, and we felt that this book would not be complete, and would hardly be justified, without giving some indication of these uses.

In the first instance computers were seen by many enterprises as aids to their accounting. Authorities in local government, for example, were one of the first such users. Each year with their large income from such local taxes as rates, and expenditure on a wide variety of things from teachers' salaries to refuse collection, anything which could streamline their accounting was welcomed with open arms.

PAYROLL

A local authority with 20,000 employees to pay weekly or monthly needs to have stored in a readily accessible form information on all these employees relating to their national insurance contributions, income tax, pension schemes, rates of pay, and so on. In the past this required a whole library of files, but with a computer this is stored magnetically on a tape or disc, which can store several million characters each. If any of this information changes, such as the tax code number of an employee, it can be updated on the tape by punching a card indicating the change and using the computer with a standard program.

Variable information such as the number of hours worked overtime and travelling expenses is punched onto cards each week and the computer combines this information with that already stored to produce a payslip and cheque in a readable form (using a line printer) for each employee.

The program for a payroll may take a team of people many months to prepare initially for an organization as complex as a local authority,

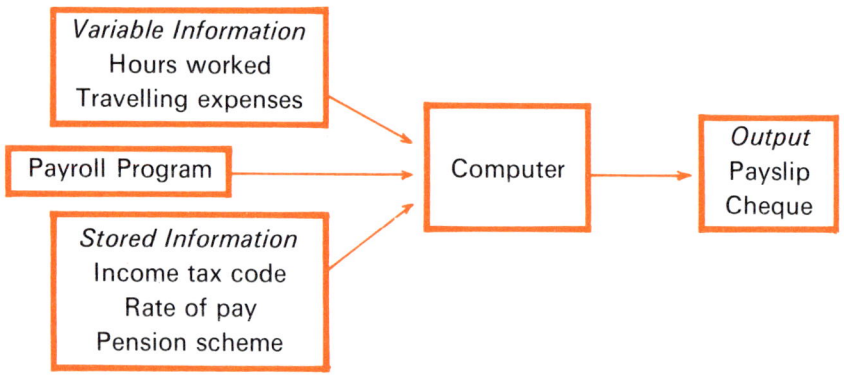

but it will then be used over and over again with little if any modification. Apart from producing the visible output of payslips it must update all the stored information such as total salary earned to date and total tax paid.

In a use of this kind the computer is not doing any complicated mathematics but acting as a very efficient accountant and using its ability to organize and process stored data to produce a payroll in a fraction of the time it would take a skilled team of human accountants.

The tapes and discs used for storing the information on the employees are not part of the computer itself but of the peripheral equipment. In a commercial computer system these *backing stores* as they are called form a major part of the system for, unlike scientific uses where the data used is always changing, there is usually a lot of relatively fixed information to be stored.

RATES AND ACCOUNTS

As well as storing information on its employees, a local authority will collect information on all its ratepayers and their property and store this in a backing store. The computer can then be programmed to work out the rates due from each individual and produce the rate demands duly addressed. As the rates are paid the stored information is updated so that when the time comes for a second or final demand only the outstanding creditors will be notified.

This kind of data processing is common to many organizations from insurance companies to gas and electricity boards. With the latter, the stored information on each customer will include such information as his tariff, agreements for servicing and payments on an appliance, while the latest meter reading gives the variable information required for the computer to print the quarterly bill.

A bank often uses a large central computer system to service many branches. All the information relating to the accounts of the customers of these branches will be stored on tapes or discs and regularly updated. Cheques these days have customers' codes printed on them in special ink which can be read directly by an input device for the computer, this does away with the intermediate and time-consuming process of punching cards and enables cheques to be cleared very quickly.

ELECTORAL REGISTRATION

Some local authorities are now compiling information on all their electorate which will be put onto a magnetic disc file and offers many possibilities. For example, the medical officer may want to do a cervical cancer check on all the women in a certain age range and the extent of such a survey can be readily found by using the computer to determine the numbers of such women living in each region. The director of education may have to decide where to spend his limited funds on building new schools and the statistics on which to base his decision would be readily accessible.

The initial compilation of the register may take a lot of effort but once this has been done the ease and speed with which stored information can be updated and processed makes decision making and the organization of the authority a case of scientific planning rather than inspired guesswork.

Police already use a computer to deal with crime statistics and the analysis of traffic accidents, while research is being made into medical diagnosis by computer. A computer could be stored with all the known facts relating to common diseases and programmed so that when fed with the symptoms of a particular patient it could suggest the possible disease, give other symptoms to expect and the best treatment. For this to work effectively each person will have a medical card punched with such information as: allergy to penicillin, blood group, diabetic, and so on, which will influence the computer's output.

STOCK CONTROL

Many large industrial and commercial enterprises require to have a lot of their available capital tied up in stock (compare the shopkeeper on a small scale) and it is important for the smooth running of their affairs that they do not run out of some vital raw material or product. On the other hand it is unprofitable to store more than is strictly required. To keep a watch on stock levels and arrange the re-ordering of stock is a job which a computer can be programmed to do very well.

In some situations such as that of a wholesaler who stocks a large variety of items in a warehouse and daily delivers his goods around the countryside by lorry in response to the orders which come in, the computer can be programmed to organize the whole process. The day's orders are given to the computer which sorts the information into the kind of stock required, decides where in the warehouse it is to be found, produces lists for the warehousemen giving the most efficient way to collect the items, and then lists for the delivery lorries as well as updating a customer's account and producing a monthly bill. (The replacement of stock is also dealt with, of course.) This is carried to the ultimate extreme in automatic warehouses where conveyor belts and fork-lift trucks are controlled by the computer to automatically collect the goods from the warehouse and deliver them to the departure bay.

Airlines use computers to store information relating to the spare parts of their planes so that if, say, a plane has a faulty engine at Nairobi the geographical location of the nearest spare part can be found and transport arranged. In addition the airline's computer stores information on all its flights and bookings.

All the uses of a computer mentioned so far have required the storage of large quantities of information which needs to be readily accessible and easily updated. The programs in most cases are long and would have taken a team of systems analysts and programmers many months to produce. The calculations are trivial and much of the programs will be concerned with locating the required information in a backing store and operating the other peripheral equipment. For example, if the output is to be on a line printer in columns spaced in a certain way then this has to be 'spelled out' precisely in the program.

This contrasts with the scientific use of a computer where the amount of data is frequently small and the calculation fairly lengthy.

MANAGEMENT

In many large contracts such as the building of an oil-tanker, or the construction of big new roads such as motorways, there are many stages in the work which depend on previous stages being completed or certain parts or materials being available on site. Before a contract is begun these stages are analysed in detail and the time it will take to complete each is estimated. From this it is possible to give a completion date for a contract, but this will only be kept if the individual time schedules on certain critical stages are maintained. The information relating to the stages, their interdependence, and estimated time of completion are stored on a tape and the computer is regularly fed with information showing the state of the project. If one stage gets behind schedule then the computer is programmed to find out how best to organize the available labour force to make up the lost time. This process is known as *critical path analysis* and the reader is recommended to read *Management and Mathematics* by Fletcher and Clarke for a fuller account of the technique.

Another important technique available to management is *linear programming*. The resources of a firm such as its labour force, raw materials, machinery, factory size together with its products, for example, can be expressed as a set of linear inequalities. These can be analysed by using a computer and a suitable program to decide how to use the resources to maximize output or maximize profits or alternatively to decide where best to invest money to improve future prospects.

Transportation is a problem which particularly faces companies whose products are bulky, such as oil companies or mining concerns. Their situation is that they have sources of raw materials at A, B, C, . . . and outlets at X, Y, Z, . . . The outputs from A, B, C, . . . , the requirements of X, Y, Z, . . . , and the costs of transporting the materials between the two are known, and the problem is to minimize the costs. The situation can be represented as a set of mathematical equations which a computer can be programmed to analyse and decide how best to distribute the materials. With an oil company the situation is further complicated by having to first send the raw materials to a refinery. The position of the refinery will greatly influence the final transport costs, and oil companies do a lot of analysis with the aid of a computer before deciding where to site a new refinery.

This chapter has left much unsaid but it is hoped that the reader will have gained some idea of the nature and widespread use of computers. Computers have been programmed to play chess, compose music, translate books, organize school timetables, mark examinations, and guide rockets to the moon. If men are to make full use of the computer in the future it is up to us to provide everyone with a basic understanding of what a computer is and what it can and cannot do, for increasingly our lives will be governed by it.

solutions to exercises

EXERCISE 1

1(a) 27+27+15   (b) 524+263−651   (c) 52+52+52+52+52

2(a)

```
Clear all registers
  217           S
       1
  519           S
       1
  Output        A
```

(b)

```
Clear all registers
  413           S
       1
  256           S
       1
  Output        A
```

(c)

```
Clear all registers
   34           S
       4
  Output        A
```

(d)

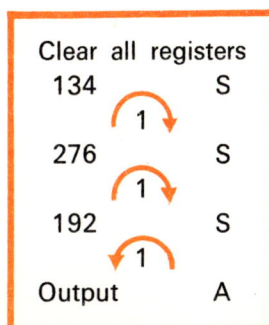

70 SOLUTIONS TO EXERCISES

EXERCISE 2

(a)
```
Clear all registers
261           S
    7
Output        A
```

(b)
```
Clear all registers
53            S
    5
71            S
    1
Output        A
```

(c)
```
Clear all registers
417           S
    23
479           S
    1
257           S
    1
Output        A
```

EXERCISE 3

1(a) 417+291 (b) 256−147
(c) 17+19−21 (d) 15+15+15=3×15

2(a)
A := 0
C := 0
S := 214
A := A+S ⎤
C := C+1 ⎦
S := 376
A := A+S ⎤
C := C+1 ⎦
Output A

(b)
A := 0
C := 0
S := 199
A := A+S ⎤
C := C+1 ⎦
S := 22
A := A−S ⎤
C := C−1 ⎦
Output A

(c)
A := 0
S := 45
A := A+S ⎤
C := C+1 ⎦
A := A+S ⎤
C := C+1 ⎦
S := 27
A := A−S ⎤
C := C−1 ⎦
Output A

SOLUTIONS TO EXERCISES

EXERCISE 4

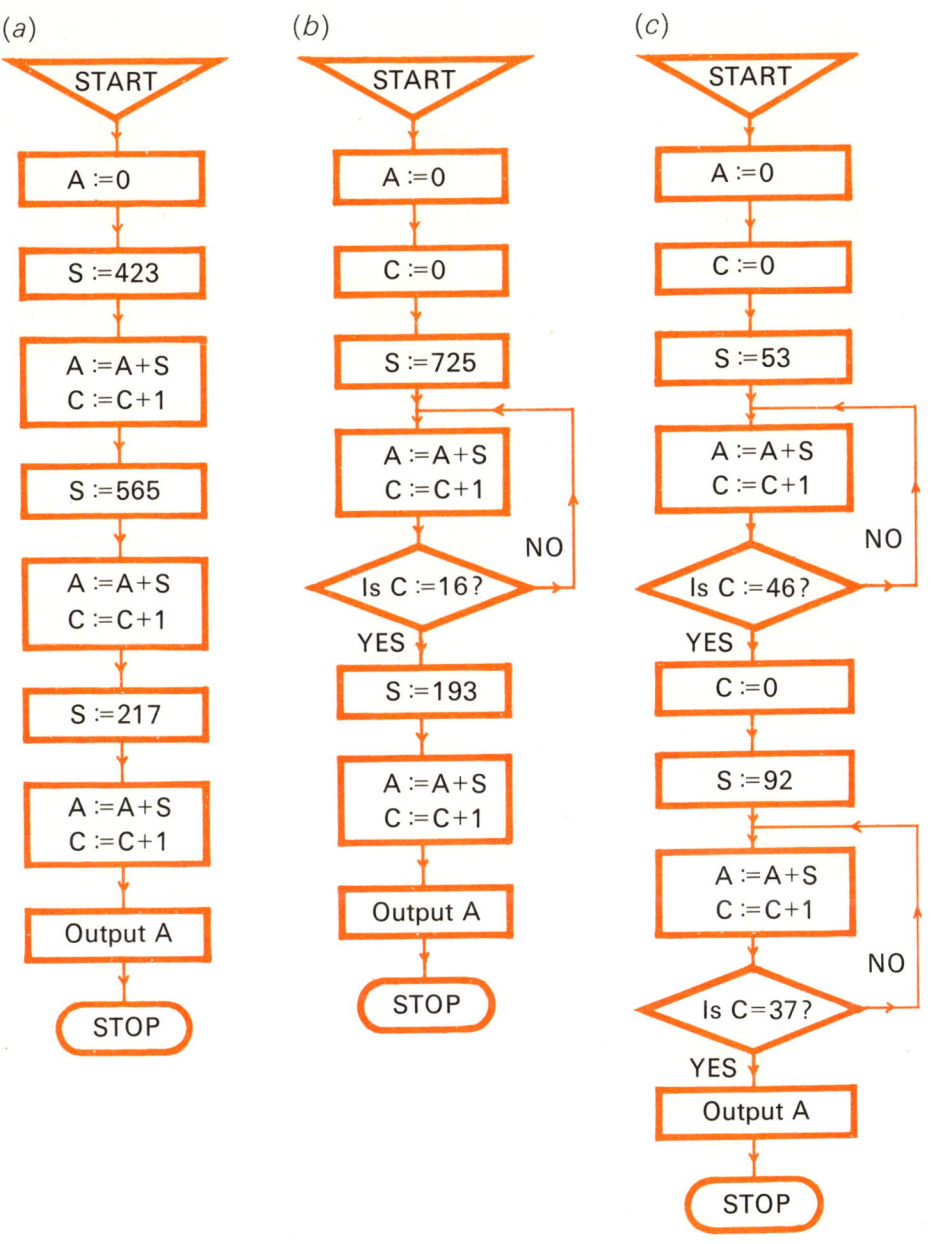

72 SOLUTIONS TO EXERCISES

EXERCISE 5

1(a) (b) (c)

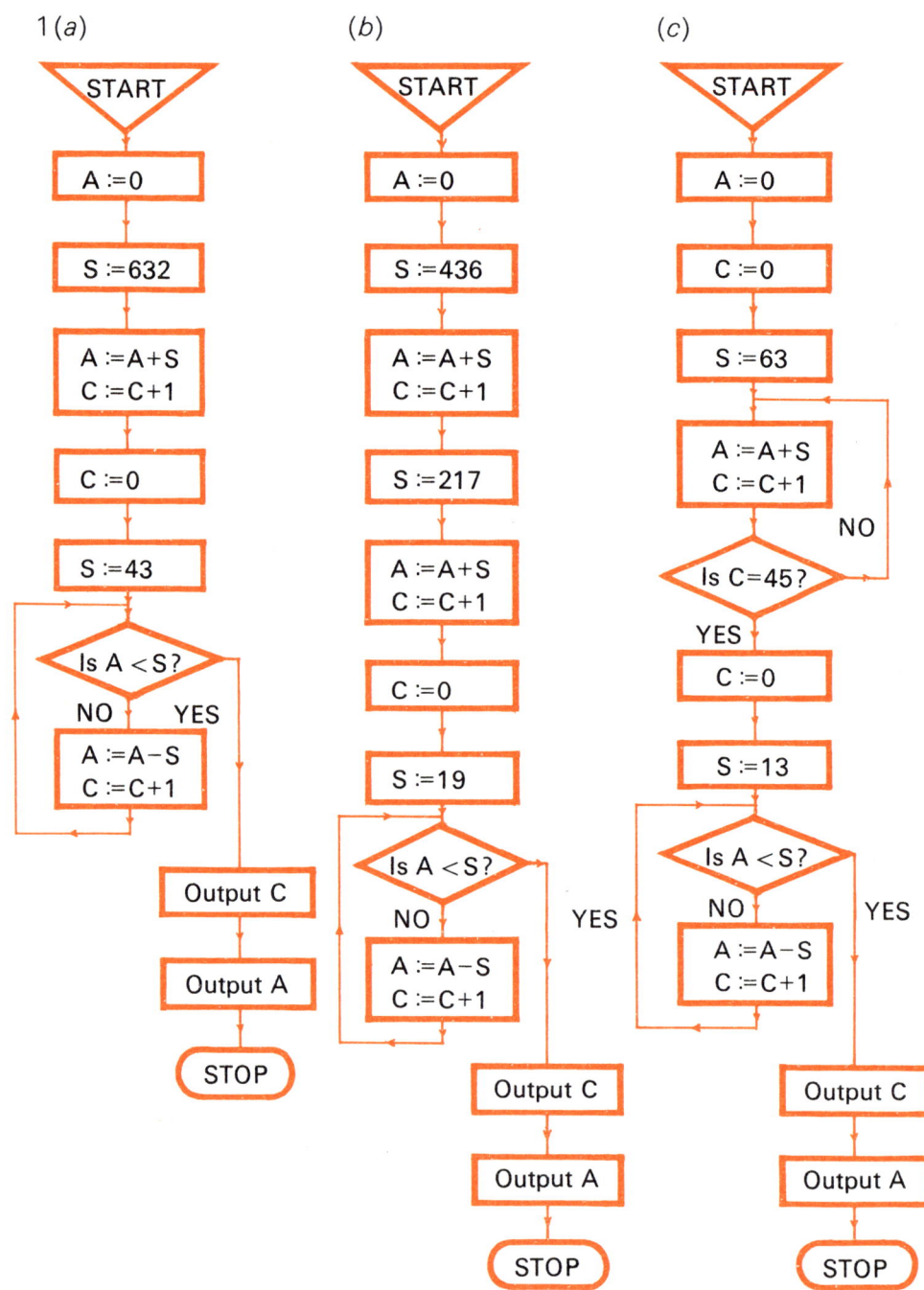

SOLUTIONS TO EXERCISES   73

EXERCISE 5 *(continued)*

2 figure 5 Program for Quotient of $120 \div 37$; figure 6 Program for n^3

EXERCISE 7

(a) 5, 15, 6   (b) 1, 3, 0   (c) 2, 3, 4   (d) 4, 3, 2   (e) 25, 9, 16

EXERCISE 8

1 (a)
S1 := Tape (2639)
S2 := Tape (173)
S3 := Tape (786)
S4 := Tape (254)
S1 := S1 × S2
S3 := S3 − S4
S1 := S1 ÷ S3
Print S1

(b)
S1 := Tape (2·83)
S2 := Tape (3·96)
S3 := S2 × S2
S3 := S1 + S3
S1 := S1 × S1
S1 := S1 − S2
S1 := S1 ÷ S3
Print S1

(c) The calculation carried out would not be the one required

2
S1 := Tape (1·932)
S2 := S1 × S1
S2 := S2 × S2
S1 := S1 × S2
Print S1

3 (a)
S1 := Tape (x)
S2 := Tape (y)
S3 := S1 + S2
S1 := S1 − S2
S1 := S3 ÷ S1
Print S1

(b)
S1 := Tape (x)
S2 := Tape (y)
S3 := S1 × S1
S3 := S3 × S2
S3 := S3 − S1
S3 := S3 + S2
S1 := S1 × S2
S1 := S3 ÷ S1
Print S1

(c)
S1 := Tape (x)
S2 := Tape (y)
S3 := S1 × S1
S4 := S2 × S2
S5 := S3 × S4
S5 := S5 + S1
S5 := S5 + S2
S1 := S3 + S4
S1 := S5 ÷ S1
Print S1

(d) The formula in (c) is unchanged when x and y are interchanged

74 SOLUTIONS TO EXERCISES

EXERCISE 8 (continued)

4
S1 := Tape (x)   or   S1 := Tape (x)
S2 := Tape (2)   S2 := S1 × S1
S3 := S1 + S2   S3 := S1 ÷ S1
S4 := S1 × S1   S3 := S3 + S3
S3 := S3 − S4   S3 := S3 + S1
S4 := S4 × S1   S3 := S3 − S2
S4 := S4 × S2   S2 := S2 × S1
S4 := S4 + S3   S2 := S2 + S2
Print S4   S3 := S3 + S2
                       Print S3

5 (a)
    START
(1) S2 := 0
(2) S3 := 0
┌▶(3) S1 := Tape
│ (4) S2 := S2 + S1
│ (5) S3 := S3 + 1
└─(6) If more data jump to (3)
(7) S1 := S2 ÷ S3
(8) Print S1
    STOP

(b) 3 locations unless all the data is input first when more are required

6
START
S1 := Tape (a)
S2 := Tape (b)
S3 := Tape (c)
S4 := Tape (d)
S1 := S1 × S4
S2 := S2 × S3
S1 := S1 − S2
Print S1
STOP

7
START
S1 := Tape (a)
S2 := Tape (b)
S3 := Tape (p)
S4 := Tape (r)
S5 := S1 × S3
S6 := S2 × S4
S5 := S5 + S6
Print S5

S5 := Tape (q)
S6 := Tape (s)
S1 := S1 × S5
S2 := S2 × S6
S1 := S1 + S2
Print S1
S1 := Tape (c)
S2 := Tape (d)
S3 := S1 × S3

S4 := S2 × S4
S3 := S3 + S4
Print S3
S5 := S1 × S5
S6 := S2 × S6
S5 := S5 + S6
Print S5
STOP

EXERCISE 9

    START
(1) S3 := 0
┌▶(2) S1 := Tape (x)
│ (3) S2 := S1 × S1
│ (4) S2 := S2 × S1
│ (5) S3 := S3 + S2
└─(6) If more data jump to (2)
(7) Print S3
    STOP

SOLUTIONS TO EXERCISES

EXERCISE 10

1(a)
```
        START
(1)     S1 := 0
(2)     S2 := Tape (x)
(3)     S1 := S1 + S2
(4)     If more data jump to (2)
(5)     S1 := S1 × S1
(6)     Print S1
        STOP
```

(b)
```
        START
(1)     S1 := 0
(2)     S2 := 0
(3)     S3 := Tape (x)
(4)     S1 := S1 + S3
(5)     S3 := S3 × S3
(6)     S2 := S2 + S3
(7)     If more data jump to (3)
(8)     S1 := S1 × S2
(9)     Print S1
        STOP
```

(c)
```
        START
(1)     S1 := 0
(2)     S2 := Tape (x)
(3)     S3 := Tape (y)
(4)     S1 := S1 + S2
(5)     S1 := S1 − S3
(6)     If more data jump to (2)
(7)     Print S1
        STOP
```

(d)
```
        START
(1)     S1 := 1
(2)     S2 := 0
(3)     S4 := 0
(4)     S2 := S2 + S1
(5)     S3 := S1 ÷ S2
(6)     S4 := S4 + S3
(7)     If S2 < 200 jump to (4)
(8)     Print S4
        STOP
```

2
```
        START
(1)     S1 := Tape (2·6934)
(2)     S2 := S1 × S1
(3)     S3 := Tape (2)
(4)     S2 := S2 × S1
(5)     S3 := S3 + 1
(6)     If S2 < 1000 jump to (4)
(7)     Print S3
        STOP
```

3 Number is the least power of 3 to exceed 100

SOLUTIONS TO EXERCISES

EXERCISE 10 *(continued)*

4
```
       START
 (1)   S1 := Tape (1)
 (2)   S2 := Tape (2)
 (3)   S3 := Tape (−1)
 (4)   S4 := Tape (0)
→(5)   S3 := S3+S2
 (6)   S5 := S1÷S3
 (7)   S4 := S4+S5
 (8)   S3 := S3+S2
 (9)   S5 := S1÷S3
(10)   S4 := S4−S5
(11)   If S3 < 3999 jump to (5)
(12)   S4 := S4×S2
(13)   S4 := S4×S2
(14)   Print S4
       STOP
```

5
```
       START
 (1)   S3 := 0
 (2)   S4 := 0
 (3)   S5 := 0
→(4)   S1 := Tape (x)
 (5)   S2 := Tape (y)
 (6)   S6 := S1×S2
 (7)   S5 := S5+S6
 (8)   S1 := S1×S1
 (9)   S2 := S2×S2
(10)   S3 := S3+S1
(11)   S4 := S4+S2
(12)   If more data jump to (4)
(13)   S3 := S3×S4
(14)   Print S3
(15)   Print S5
       STOP
```

6
```
       START
 (1)   S1 := 1
 (2)   S2 := 0
 (3)   S3 := Tape (r)
 (4)   S4 := Tape (100)
 (5)   S5 := Tape (c)
 (6)   S6 := Tape (n)
 (7)   S3 := S3÷S4
 (8)   S5 := S5÷S3
 (9)   S3 := S3+S1
→(10)  S1 := S1×S3
(11)   S2 := S2+1
(12)   If S2 < S6 jump to (10)
(13)   S1 := S1−1
(14)   S1 := S1×S5
(15)   Print S1
       STOP
```

further reading

SCHOOLS' TEXTS
School Mathematics Project: Books 3, 4, and *Advanced Mathematics Book 3*. C.U.P.
Contemporary School Mathematics: Computing I, and II. Arnold.
Mathematics—A New Approach: Book 4, by Mansfield and Bruckheimer. Chatto and Windus.
Computing in Mathematics, edited by J. D. Tinsley. S.M.P.
Some Lessons in Mathematics, edited by T. J. Fletcher. C.U.P.

PROGRAMMING
Elementary Programming and Algol, by K. Nicol. McGraw-Hill.
Practical Programming, by P. N. Corlett and J. D. Tinsley. S.M.P. Handbook. C.U.P.

COMPUTERS
We Built Our Own Computers. S.M.P. Handbook. C.U.P.
Thinking Machines, by Adler. Dobson.
Electronic Computers, by Hollingdale and Toothill. Pelican.
Digital Computers, by Marchant and Pegg. Blackie.

GENERAL BACKGROUND
An Introduction to Computing, by Wooldridge. O.U.P.
Management and Mathematics, by Fletcher and Clarke. Business Publications.
Mathematics in Management, by A. Battersby. Pelican.
The Age of Automation, by Sir Leon Bagrit. Weidenfeld & Nicolson.
High Speed Computing: Methods and Applications, by Hollingdale. E.U.P.
An Introduction to Computational Methods, by Redish. E.U.P.
Numerical Methods and Computing, by Noble. Oliver & Boyd.

COMPUTER EDUCATION
The bulletin of the Computer Education Group of the British Computer Society. 5s. per year from Mrs P. Jackson, C.E.G. Treasurer, Staffordshire College of Technology, Beaconside, Stafford, Staffs.

index

accumulator 3, 8
address 32
Algol 32
arithmetic unit 22, 27, 52
autocode 31
automatic warehouse 66
average 41

backing store 64
binary operations 35

carriage shift 7
character 24
class computer 51
compiler 31, 57
computer system 26, 64
control unit 22, 28, 52
counter 3, 5, 8, 40
critical path analysis 67

data link 46
data processing 30, 64
data store 51
decision box 12, 47
desk calculator 1
differential equation 62
disc pack 25
dry check 15, 33

e^x 59
electoral registration 64

ferrite core matrix store 28
Fibonacci 55
flow diagram 11, 47
Fortran 32

graph plotter 26 58

Hero 53, 56

input 1, 51
input instruction 34, 53
input unit 21
integrated circuits 27
integration 62
iterative procedures 61

jump 38
jump instruction 38, 41, 53

K (32K) 29

letter shift 23
library of programs 40, 59
linear equations 62, 67
linear programming 67
line printer 27
log x 59
loop 12

machine code 31
magnetic disc 24
magnetic tape 24
management 67
modulus 55

Olivetti Programma 101 45, 46
output instructions 34
output unit 21, 52

paper stores 18
paper tape 23
payroll 63

INDEX

peripheral equipment 26, 64
polynomial 58
program 3
program store 37, 51
punched cards 23,

rates 64
reading head 24
register 3

setting register 3, 8
sine *x* 59
software 40

square root 56
standard deviation 40
stock control 66
storage location 32, 37, 52
store unit 28
subroutine 59
systems analyst 66

tape punch 20, 24
tape reader 20, 24
transportation 67

update 63, 64